IMPROVING
YOUR
REASONING

So necessary is it that, when a thing is talked of, there should be a name to call it by; so conducive, not to say necessary, to the prevalence of reason and common sense and moral honesty, that instruments of deception should be talked of, well talked of, and talked out of fashion—in a word, talked down, that . . . the author has struck out under the spur of necessity a separate barbarism for each of these fallacies.

Jeremy Bentham

IMPROVING YOUR REASONING

Alex C. Michalos

Department of Philosophy
University of Pittsburgh

PRENTICE-HALL, INC.
Englewood Cliffs, New Jersey

© 1970 by PRENTICE-HALL, INC.
Englewood Cliffs, N. J.

All rights reserved. No part of this book
may be reproduced in any form or by any means
without permission in writing from the publisher.

C 13-453464-6
P 13-453456-5

Library of Congress Catalog Card No.: 71–102286

Current printing (last digit):
10

Printed in the United States of America

PRENTICE-HALL INTERNATIONAL, INC., *London*
PRENTICE-HALL OF AUSTRALIA, PTY. LTD., *Sydney*
PRENTICE-HALL OF CANADA, LTD., *Toronto*
PRENTICE-HALL OF INDIA PRIVATE LIMITED, *New Delhi*
PRENTICE-HALL OF JAPAN, INC., *Tokyo*

for my gentle daughter Cynthia
my easygoing son Ted
and my independent daughter Stephanie

PREFACE

This book has been written for all who are interested in sound thinking, whether college students or people with no previous training in logic, very little spare time, and a mild interest in learning how to distinguish good arguments from bad ones. Hopefully, it may help them learn the differences between those types of arguments that actually prove what they are supposed to prove and those that do not. The latter types are not only fallacious and deceptive, but too often extremely harmful, since they may lead to erroneous conclusions which become the bases of foolish actions that may frequently have disastrous consequences for them and for innocent bystanders as well.

The book is divided into eight chapters. In the first chapter we consider the basic (formal) structures of some frequently used types of good arguments. We examine in detail the fundamental distinction between arguments which are bad because they have faulty "logical skeletons" and arguments which are bad because they have false premises. In Chapter Two we discuss additional types of bad arguments which we call irrelevant or circular, including seven types of circularity. Chapters Three and Four elucidate thirty-seven types of arguments that are more or less irrelevant to the claims they are supposed to establish.

The remaining chapters contain discussions of arguments which are frequently irrelevant but sometimes fallacious or deceptive for vaguer reasons. In the fifth chapter, for example, we consider arguments whose most distinctive features are their tendencies to create confusion. The following chapter is about blunders that arise when we are classifying things into different groups. In Chapter Seven we examine political fallacies; these include a number of misleading tactics or maneuvers that shrewd but dishonest leaders and aspirants to leadership have been known to use against others. The final chapter is concerned with mistakes that arise when arguments must take into account uncertainty, statistics, and probability.

I certainly do not recommend the memorization of all ninety-three of these species. That would be extremely time consuming and not obviously profitable. Instead, I suggest that you merely try to "think your way through" the discussions, definitions, and examples, to grasp the *kinds* of errors or deceptive tactics introduced, and *most importantly* to identify instances of their occurrence in your own experience. The latter is an extremely effective and interesting way to master logical principles. Once you have caught yourself or someone else falling prey to the fallacies considered here, you will be less likely to fall again.

Finally, it should be noted that the symbolic-mathematical notation characteristic of most modern logic texts has been kept to a bare minimum here. Moreover, technical terms are introduced and defined only when it seems that a new word may be useful to isolate and elucidate a new idea. For rapid reviews of the material, over 600 short answer problems, with solutions, have been included.

University of Pittsburgh   ALEX C. MICHALOS

CONTENTS

chapter
five

CONFUSION, 70

chapter
eight

INDUCTIVE FALLACIES, 106

IMPROVING YOUR REASONING

chapter
one ARGUMENTS

Give instruction to a wise man,
and he will be yet wiser. Proverbs 9 :9

1.1 Deductive and inductive arguments

Some people argue about everything. Some people never give you an
argument. People who argue about everything are a pain in the neck.
(Sometimes they are called 'philosophers'.) People who never argue about
anything are wishy-washy. They are wishy-washy because some things
should be argued. Some things are worth proving. Some things are worth
fighting for, even if the only weapons used are words.

You have been in arguments. You know how disturbing they can be.
You know how uncontrollable they can be, and you know how embar-
rassing they can be. If you are lucky, you know how enlightening they
can be. There is nothing like a good argument to clear the air. Sometimes
nothing else can do the job.

Now just what *is* an argument? Think back. How would you characterize your last argument? The last big argument I had was with a neighbor
whose dog kept turning over our garbage can. My neighbor gave me hell
for not buying a cover for my can. And I gave him the same for not keeping his dumb dog off my back porch. It was a pretty grim display of
nastiness on both sides. But that gives you some idea of what I mean by an
argument.

Let's take a closer look at this argument. Here is my neighbor's claim.
Call him 'Able'.

> Able : If your garbage can had a cover then my dog would not
> be tempted to get into your garbage. So, if you want my dog to
> stay out of your garbage then loosen up and buy a lousy cover.

My claim ran like this (I will be 'Baker').

> Baker : If you kept your dog tied up (or well-fed, or on your own
> property) then he could not get into my garbage. So, if you don't
> want your dog eating my garbage then take care of him the way
> you should.

All very touching, I'm sure. But never mind the sentiment. There are a few lessons to be learned from this exchange. In the first place, notice that Able and Baker both expressed their views using *two declarative* or *assertive* sentences. Those are the only kind of sentences we will consider, because those are the only kind that can be true or false. Notice also that the second sentence of each person begins with the word 'so'. This little word 'so' has a very important role to play. It might have been played by 'thus', 'hence', or 'therefore'. What is that role? Just this: 'So' tells us that whatever comes next *comes from* whatever came first. Or, to put this important point another way; 'so' tells us that the sentence following it is supposed to follow from the sentence preceding it *according to some logical rule*. Or, in other words; 'so' tells us that the sentence following it is the *conclusion* of an argument and that the sentence preceding it is the *premiss* of that argument.

In the last sentence we introduced a sense of the word *argument* that is slightly different from the sense of that word which was used earlier. Earlier we were talking about the kind of arguments that people can *have with* other people. These are verbal scraps, linguistic battles, or fights with words. But in the last sentence of the last paragraph we were talking about the kind of arguments that people can *present to* other people. These **arguments** are sequences of sentences divided in such a way that some of the sentences are supposed to be the reason, justification, guarantee, warrant, or support for some other sentence in the sequence. The sentences that provide the reason or warrant are called **premisses.** The sentence that is supposed to be warranted by the premisses is called the **conclusion.**

The arguments presented above by Able and Baker each have only one premiss. This is not necessary. Arguments can have any number of premisses. Here are two more examples:

(premisses) $\left\{\begin{array}{l}\text{If Fred's car is out of gasoline then its}\\ \text{motor will not run.}\\ \text{Fred's car is out of gasoline.}\end{array}\right.$

(conclusion)   Therefore, its motor will not run.

(premisses)   {Most two-year-old children are stubborn.
                Roger's daughter is two years old.

(conclusion)   Hence, it is probable that Roger's daughter
                is stubborn.

Both of these arguments have two premisses. In this respect they are alike. There is, however, an important *logical* difference between the first and the second. It is a difference that is revealed by the warning phrase

It is probable that

which is prefaced to the conclusion of the second argument. This phrase is used in order to *warn* us that the conclusion

Roger's daughter is stubborn.

is not completely certain relative to the given premisses. The conclusion is *supposed* to be more or less *probable* relative to those premisses, but that is about all. This is quite different from the claim made about the conclusion of the first argument. *That* conclusion is *supposed* to be *certain* relative to the given premisses.

An argument whose conclusion is supposed, alleged, or claimed to be certain relative to its premisses is called **deductive**. Even if the argument has an error in it and does not do what it is supposed to do, we call it 'deductive'. Calling it 'deductive' does not make it good or bad. It just tells everyone what is to be expected of it. The first argument (about Fred's car) is deductive.

An argument whose conclusion is supposed, alleged, or claimed to be more or less acceptable relative to its premisses is called **inductive**. Even if the argument has an error in it and does not do what it is supposed to do, we call it 'inductive'. Calling it 'inductive' does not make it good or bad. It just tells everyone what is to be expected of it. The second argument (about Roger's daughter) is inductive.

Notice that our definition of an 'inductive argument' contains the word *acceptable* rather than the word *probable*. The former is merely more general. Usually the conclusion of an inductive argument is described as more or less probable relative to its premisses. But sometimes it is described as more or less likely, well supported, well confirmed, reasonable, useful, sensible, and so on. That is, there are *many* ways to characterize the *relation* that obtains between the premisses and the conclusion of an inductive argument. So, it seems preferable to use the vaguer term *acceptable* in our definition.

Here are two more examples:

| (premisses) | All chickens are birds. |
| (conclusion) | Hence, the neck of a chicken is the neck of a bird. |

| (premisses) | The weather in January is usually similar to that in February. It was cold in January. |
| (conclusion) | So, it is likely that it will be cold in February. |

The first argument leaves *no* room for doubt. The conclusion is supposed to follow from the premiss

All chickens are birds.

with complete certainty, and it does. However, even if it *didn't*, we would say that the argument is deductive. We say that it is deductive merely because we know that it is *supposed, claimed, intended,* or *alleged* to establish its conclusion

The neck of a chicken is the neck of a bird.

with complete certainty. That is, *relative to* or *given* that premiss, we are supposed to be completely stuck with, committed to, or unable to escape from that conclusion. Whether or not the argument does what it is supposed to do and we are in fact stuck with that conclusion is another question.

The second argument *leaves* room for doubt. The conclusion is supposed to be more or less *likely* relative to the premisses

The weather in January is usually
similar to that in February.
It was cold in January.

and it is. However, even if it *weren't*, we would say that the argument is inductive. We say that it is inductive merely because we know that it is *supposed, claimed, intended* or *alleged* to make its conclusion

It will be cold in February.

more or less likely, hence, *acceptable.* That is, *relative to* or *given* those premises, we are supposed to be more or less (but not completely) stuck with, committed to, or unable to escape from that conclusion. Whether or not the argument does what it is supposed to do and we are in fact more or less stuck with that conclusion is another question.

Now, if we define **logic** as the study of arguments and things directly related to them (like, say, sentences and terms of various sorts), then we must say that this study may be divided into two main parts, namely deduction and induction. In **deductive logic** or deduction we concentrate on principles that are primarily applicable to deductive arguments. In **inductive logic** or induction we concentrate on principles that are primarily applicable to inductive arguments.

Why should anyone be interested in the study of logic? As my brother used to say, "You can't put logic in the bank!" The most persuasive answer I can give to this question is this: Whether you study logic or not, you *must* use it. You cannot avoid it. *No rational person can avoid using logic.* If you try to convince me that you can avoid it, you will have to present an *argument.* Then you will be using logic. See what I mean? You can't avoid logic.

The last paragraph should have put things in a new light. The question is: Will you study logic in order to learn *more* about this tool you have been using for years and will continue to use? Or, will you ignore the study of logic and continue to use it anyhow? The choice is yours. So are the consequences. (That is supposed to sound threatening.)

Review problems for Sec. 1.1

1. What is logic?
2. What is the difference between inductive and deductive logic?
3. What is an argument?
4. What are the main parts of an argument?
5. Make up examples of an inductive and a deductive argument.

1.2   Valid and invalid arguments

If you are still with me, then you are probably interested in learning more about arguments. If you are, then I would bet my bicycle that what you would really like to know is how to distinguish the good ones from the bad ones. How can we tell which arguments are doing what they are supposed to do and which are not? The answer to this question is a very very long story, but the book in your hands contains a few of the most *useful* chapters. At least I *think* they will be the most useful *to you*.

Consider the following deductive arguments:

> All cats are animals.
> All tigers are cats.
> So, all tigers are animals.

> All humans are mortal.
> All Greeks are humans.
> So, all Greeks are mortal.

Each of these arguments is about different things. The first is about animals, cats, and tigers; the second, about mortals, humans, and Greeks. Arguments that are about different things are said to have different **contents**. So, these arguments have different contents. But they have the very same logical *form*, *pattern*, or *structure*. The pattern of each of these arguments is this:

> All _____ are _ _ _.
> All . . . are _____ .
> So, all . . . are _ _ _.

The only words occurring in this skeleton are logical guides called **operators**. You already know how the word 'so' operates. It tells us that what follows it is a conclusion. The words 'all' and 'are' tell us that everything following the former is in the same class as everything following the latter. For example,

> *All* cats *are* animals.

tells us that every cat belongs to the class of animals. Similarly,

> *All* Greeks *are* mortal.

tells us that every Greek is also something mortal.

> All _____ are _ _ _.

appears over and over in logic. It is called a **sentence schema** (form, pattern, skeleton, or structure). The plural of 'schema' is 'schemata'. There are *many* different types of sentence schemata, some of which we will consider in the next section. When the solid and broken lines are replaced by general terms like 'man', 'clown', 'Canadian', etc., the result is an ordinary sentence.

Similarly, the pattern

All ____ are _ _ _.
All . . . are ____.
So, all . . . are _ _ _.

appears repeatedly in logic. It is *one* of many patterns known as **argument schemata** (forms or skeletons). When the solid, broken, and dotted lines are replaced by general terms, the result is an ordinary argument. This particular argument schema was identified over two thousand years ago, and it later became known as **Barbara.** We cannot go into the reasons for calling this pattern 'Barbara', but that is what every logician calls it, and that is what we will call it.

Why is Barbara so important? Barbara is important because no matter what terms we put in place of the solid, broken, and dotted lines (so long as we are consistent), *if* the premises are true then the conclusion *must* be true. That is, so long as we replace the solid line with the same term in both premises, the broken line with the same term and the dotted line with the same term, *if* the premises are true then the conclusion *must* be true. Barbara is "absolutely loyal" in the sense that "she" never allows us to draw a false conclusion from true premises.

An argument schema is called **valid** if, and only if, it *must* yield a true conclusion whenever its place markers are replaced in such a way that its premises are all true. The ordinary argument obtained from a valid argument schema by consistently or uniformly replacing its place markers appropriately is called a **valid argument**. Hence, Barbara is a valid argument schema, and the two arguments obtained from it by replacing its place markers (the solid, broken, and dotted lines) with general terms ('human', 'Greek', etc.) are valid arguments. Because there is almost no limit to the number of different sets of three terms that we could substitute for the place markers in this schema, there is almost no limit to the number of different valid arguments that we may obtain from it. This is true of *every* argument schema (valid or not), i.e., there are always plenty of arguments which could be patterned after them. In the next section we will introduce a number of different valid argument schemata, each of which admits of a multitude of different arguments patterned after it.

Now, before you take another step in any direction *remember this:* When we say that an argument is *valid* we are saying something about its logical form, pattern, structure, or schema. We are *not* saying anything about its content. 'Barbara' is the name of a valid logical skeleton. Ordinary skeletons do not have any flesh, and logical skeletons do not have any content. They are never *about* anything. So, they can never be true or false. But they can be *valid*, and they can be *invalid*.

An argument schema is called **invalid** if, and only if, it is *possible* to uniformly or consistently replace its place markers in such a way that its premisses are all true and its conclusion is false. The ordinary argument obtained from an invalid argument schema by uniformly replacing its place markers appropriately is called an **invalid argument**. Examples of invalid argument schemata include:

All ____ are _ _ _.
All . . . are _ _ _.
Hence, all . . . are ____.

Some ____ are _ _ _.
Some . . . are ____.
Thus, some . . . are _ _ _.

We may *prove* that these schemata are invalid by replacing their place markers in such a way that every premiss is true, but the conclusions are false. The first schema may be proved invalid thus:

true   All dogs are animals.
true   All cats are animals.
false   Hence, all cats are dogs.

Notice that the solid line is always replaced by 'dogs', the broken line by 'animals', and the dotted line by 'cats'. That illustrates what we mean by a uniform or consistent replacement of place markers. If we replaced, say, one solid line by 'dogs' and the other by 'cats', the replacements would be nonuniform or inconsistent. Above all, notice that each premiss of this argument is true and the conclusion is false. This proves that the argument schema is invalid.

The second schema may be proved invalid thus:

> Some polygons are triangles.
> Some squares are polygons.
> Thus, some squares are triangles.

Again, the replacements are uniform, the premises are both true, and the conclusion is false. Therefore, the given schema is invalid.

Now, if you are still dubious about the difference between a valid argument schema and an invalid one, try to make Barbara's premises all true and "her" conclusion false. As long as your replacements are consistent, you will never succeed. With Barbara, the only way you can get a false conclusion is to include a false premiss. Barbara is a valid argument schema, and valid argument schemata *never* allow us to make uniform replacements with all true premises and false conclusions. Any argument schema that *does* allow such replacements is invalid.

Now that you know what a valid argument is, we can determine exactly which arguments are good and which are bad. Good arguments must be absolutely trustworthy. They must satisfy our intuitive notion of a *proof*. The technical name for such arguments is 'sound'. An argument which is patterned after a valid schema *and* has only true premises is called **sound**. The conclusions of sound (deductive) arguments are established beyond all doubt (if *anything* can be that certain). If you present an argument that is valid in the first place and has only true premises in the second, then you have proved *something*. If you have proved exactly what you tried to prove, then you have proved your point. You cannot do more. The arguments about cats, animals, and tigers and humans, mortals, and Greeks with which we began this section are both sound (deductive) arguments. Similarly, the argument about chickens and necks in the first section is sound.

An argument may be **unsound** for three different reasons: *First*, it may be patterned after an invalid schema. In that case we may say that it is **formally fallacious**. That is, it is unsound *because* there is something wrong with its logical form, pattern, schema, or structure. The arguments about cats, dogs, and animals and squares, triangles, and polygons are examples of arguments that are unsound or formally fallacious because they are patterned after invalid schemata. *Second*, it may contain a false premiss. For example,

> All trees are evergreens.
> All olive trees are trees.
> So, all olive trees are evergreens.

is unsound because its first premiss is false. There is, however, nothing wrong with its logical form. It has the valid form Barbara, but "she" is helpless against a false premiss. *Third*, it may be irrelevant or, perhaps, circular. That is, if an argument proves something that is, say, simply beside the point at issue then it must be regarded as unsound. For example, if the question at issue is whether or not the country needs a new president and someone proves that the state needs a new governor, his argument is an unsound argument on either side of the question at issue. Similarly, if someone begins his argument with the premiss

> The country needs a new president.

he will not convince any doubters. His argument will be rejected as unsound because it is circular.

We will have *much* more to say about irrelevant and circular arguments in later chapters. For now, all that is required is a rough idea of the different ways an argument can go wrong. In contrast to the first type of error which we have called a formal fallacy, we may refer to the other two types of errors as **informal fallacies**. An argument which is informally fallacious may have a perfectly good logical form, as our example with Barbara above. Informal fallacies are, in one way or another, errors that are directly related to the *content* of arguments. Of course, some dope might think up an argument that is unsound for *all* three reasons. That is, it is invalid, has a false premiss, and is completely beside the point. Stranger things have happened!

In the Middle Ages when someone wanted to express his approval of an argument he would say "*Sequitur*", meaning it (the conclusion) follows. When the conclusion did not follow from its premises he would say "*Non sequitur*". Nowadays we might express our disapproval of an argument by referring to it as a *non sequitur*, but few people would express their approval by saying "*Sequitur*". Usually we would just call it a sound argument.

The following diagram illustrates the classification of arguments we have suggested in the last two sections:

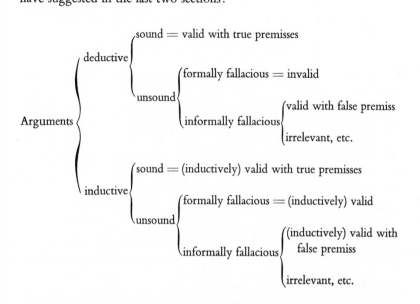

Notice that the divisions of inductive arguments are exactly like those of deductive arguments except for the word 'inductively' in front of 'valid' and 'invalid'. We have not talked about inductive validity because it is a bit more complicated than deductive validity and it would take us into some problematic issues. But for our purposes it is enough to notice that parallel distinctions arise in both areas. For example, inductive arguments may be unsound because they violate a formal principle, or because they have a false premiss, or because they are simply irrelevant to some question at issue. (If you are interested in tackling induction more thoroughly, you might pick up a copy of my *Principles of Logic*. That's not *only* a plug!)

Review problems for Sec. 1.2

I.   What is the difference between

1. sentences and sentences schemata
2. arguments and argument schemata
3. valid and invalid argument schemata

4. sound and unsound arguments
5. formal and informal fallacies?

II. Explain the three reasons one might have for calling an argument 'unsound'.
III. What is Barbara?
IV. How does one determine whether or not the place markers in a schema have been replaced in a uniform or consistent way?
V. Answer the following 'true' or 'false'. and if 'false' give a reason for your answer:

1. The premisses of a valid argument must be true.
2. Some premisses of a valid argument must be true.
3. A sound argument is an argument schema.
4. An unsound argument may be invalid.
5. A sentence schema must be true.
6. A sentence schema must be true or false.
7. An argument with only true premisses and a valid schema is sound.
8. Any argument with true premisses and a true conclusion is valid.
9. Any argument with true premisses and a true conclusion is sound.
10. The premisses of a valid argument guarantee the truth of its conclusion.
11. Invalid arguments are formally fallacious.
12. Formally fallacious arguments must be patterned after valid schemata.
13. All informally fallacious arguments have false premisses.
14. If any premiss of an argument is false, then its conclusion must be false.
15. An argument with a false premiss is informally fallacious.
16. Some valid arguments are sound.
17. A valid argument schema must be sound.

1.3 Some important valid and invalid forms: Syllogisms

We are interested in distinguishing good arguments from bad ones. That means we must distinguish sound arguments from unsound ones, and that means we must have some means of deciding which are valid and which are invalid. There are a number of *tests* that might be applied to various kinds of argument schemata to determine their validity or invalidity. Most of them involve more technicalities than we want to introduce. So, what I am going to do is present a brief catalogue of useful valid forms which thousands of students and logicians have already tested for hundreds of years.

To begin with, Barbara has fourteen first cousins. If we use '*S*', '*P*', and '*M*' instead of lines as place markers, the whole lot looks like this. (The 'so's' are omitted.)

Barbara	*Celarent*	*Darii*	*Ferio*
All M is P.	No M is P.	All M is P.	No M is P.
All S is M.	All S is M.	Some S is M.	Some S is M.
All S is P.	No S is P.	Some S is P.	Some S is not P.

Cesare	*Camestres*	*Festino*	*Baroco*
No P is M.	All P is M.	No P is M.	All P is M.
All S is M.	No S is M.	Some S is M.	Some S is not M.
No S is P.	No S is P.	Some S is not P.	Some S is not P.

Disamis	*Datisi*	*Bocardo*	*Ferison*
Some M is P.	All M is P.	Some M is not P.	No M is P.
All M is S.	Some M is S.	All M is S.	Some M is S.
Some S is P.	Some S is P.	Some S is not P.	Some S is not P.

Camenes	*Dimaris*	*Fresison*
All P is M.	Some P is M.	No P is M.
No M is S.	All M is S.	Some M is S.
No S is P.	Some S is P.	Some S is not P.

Figure 1.31

Notice that every one of these patterns has three distinct place markers, two premises, and a conclusion. Furthermore, only four types of *sentence* schemata are employed. They are called **categorical sentence schemata,** namely

> All S is P.
> No S is P.
> Some S is P.
> Some S is not P.

Arguments having these characteristics are called **syllogisms.** So now you have fifteen valid syllogistic schemata to work with.

Replacing 'M's' with 'rodents', 'P's' with 'animals', and 'S's' with 'squirrels', let us see what sorts of arguments may be obtained from some of the schemata in Figure 1.31.

The valid argument schema *Darii* yields the following *sound* argument (replacing 'is' with 'are' for grammatical reasons):

> All rodents are animals.
> Some squirrels are rodents
> So, some squirrels are animals.

This argument is sound because it has only true premises and it is patterned after the valid argument schema Darii. As a matter of fact, of course, *all* squirrels are animals and rodents. Hence, the second premiss and conclusion of this argument are weaker than they might be. Nevertheless, the weaker assertions are true too.

The valid argument schema *Cesare* yields the following *unsound* argument:

> No animals are rodents.
> All squirrels are rodents.
> So, no squirrels are animals.

This argument is unsound because its first premiss is false. It is, however, perfectly valid because it is patterned after the valid argument schema *Cesare*.

The valid argument schema *Disamis* yields the following *unsound* argument;

> Some rodents are animals.
> All rodents are squirrels.
> So, some squirrels are animals.

This argument is unsound because its second premiss is false. It is, however, perfectly valid because it is patterned after the valid argument schema *Disamis*. Notice that *unlike* the false conclusion of the argument patterned after *Cesare*, the conclusion of this argument is true. This should present no special problem. Both arguments are rejected as unsound because they have false premises. The fact that one has a true conclusion and the other a false one is simply irrelevant to the fact that both arguments are unsound.

If you are clever at noticing similarities, these fifteen forms will prove to be very useful. Let me give you an example. The following argument

> Everyone waiting for the bus
> was drenched from the rain.
> Paul was waiting for the bus.
> Therefore, Paul was drenched
> from the rain.

may be regarded as patterned after Barbara. Here is how:

> *All* persons who were waiting for the bus *are*
> persons who were drenched from the rain.

> *All* persons identical to Paul *are* persons who
> were waiting for the bus.
> Therefore, *all* persons identical to Paul *are*
> persons who were drenched from the rain.

All we did was turn phrases like

> waiting for the bus

into general terms like

> persons who were waiting for the bus.

Similarly, quantity words like 'everything', 'everyone', 'everybody' can be replaced by '*all*'; 'a few', 'many', 'most' can be replaced by '*some*', and so on. Hence, for example

> Every pretty girl is married.
> No married people are satisfied.
> So, no satisfied people are pretty girls.

would easily be recognized as an argument patterned after *Camenes*. Again,

> A few men are not Polish.
> Every man is mortal.
> So, a few mortals are not Polish.

is simply *Bocardo* with both cases of 'some' replaced by 'a few'. The following argument

> Plumbers are never mayors.
> One or two mayors are brutal.
> So, one or two brutal people are not plumbers.

may be recognized as *Fresison* with 'never' replacing 'no' and 'one or two' replacing each occurrence of 'some'.

However, even if you *are* clever, such juggling has its limits. Some valid arguments are not patterned after any syllogistic schema, and we will consider a number of illustrative cases of such arguments in the next section.

Review problems for Sec. 1.3

I. Explain the following:

1. syllogism
2. syllogistic schema
3. categorical sentence schema

II Test the following syllogisms for validity by matching their skeletons against those in Figure 1.31: (Straight lines are used to separate premisses from conclusion.)

1. Some generals are warmongers.
    All warmongers are frightening people.
    Some frightening people are generals.

2. No bipeds are octopi.
    All bipeds are light-footed animals.
    No light-footed animals are octopi.

3. No dogfish are swans.
    Some birds are swans.
    Some birds are not dogfish.

4. All polecats are fighters.
    No Siamese cats are polecats.
    No Siamese cats are fighters.

5. All philosophers are quiet.
    All powder puffs are quiet.
    All powder puffs are philosophers.

6. Some round things are bubbles.
    Some heads are round things.
    Some heads are bubbles.

7. No children are apple blossoms.
    Some children are angels.
    Some angels are not apple blossoms.

8. All werewolves need haircuts.
    Some cucumbers do not need haircuts.
    Some cucumbers are not werewolves.

9. No man is an island.
    All oases are islands.
    No oases are men.

10. Good coffee is reheatable.
    Good coffee is unbeatable.
    Reheatable coffee is unbeatable.

11. A centipede has a hundred legs.
     <u>Any bug with a hundred legs never dances.</u>
     Some centipedes never dance.
12. Some medicine tastes terrible.
     <u>No ham sandwiches taste terrible.</u>
     No medicine is a ham sandwich.

III. Usually one does not find syllogisms in nice neat packages. A conclusion may be written first, or between its premisses, or after both premisses. There are some fairly reliable signs of an intended conclusion. The words 'thus', 'therefore', 'hence', 'so', and 'it follows that' are generally signs of an intended conclusion. On the other hand, words like 'because', 'for', and 'since' are generally signs of intended premisses. By keeping these guides in mind and attending to the sense of the sentences, one can usually separate the warrant offered for a claim from the claim itself. Sometimes, of course, no clear distinction between warrant and claim has been made. In these cases there simply is no argument. Such cases may be spotted immediately by the *absence* of premiss or conclusion signs and by the abundance of conjunctions such as 'and', 'while', 'however', etc.

Decide which of the following are arguments and test them for validity by matching their patterns against those in Figure 1.31. Where there is no argument, write NA:

1. Since all birds are worm-eaters and some birds are chickens, some chickens are worm-eaters.
2. No oboes are loud and all oboes are woodwinds and some woodwinds are not loud.
3. Because all radiators are iron, some warm things are iron, since all radiators are warm.
4. Some blondes are healthy because some Germans are healthy, and all Germans are blonde.
5. No killers are kind; so, some boys are not killers, since some boys are kind.
6. All snowballs are white; so, since some coals are not white; some coals are not snowballs.
7. While no flowers are bugs and all bees are bugs, no bees are flowers.
8. No eggs are numbers, for all numbers are abstract and no eggs are abstract.
9. All poets are drunkards and some women are poets; thus, some women are drunkards.
10. All eggs are breakable but all chickens are not eggs and all chickens are not breakable.
11. Some oilmen are not rich; hence, because all oilmen are Texans, some Texans are not rich.
12. As no rugs are Islamic and some rugs are woven, it follows that some woven things are not Islamic.

1.4   More valid and invalid forms: Nonsyllogisms

In Sec. 1.3 we introduced fifteen valid argument schemata, each of which involved some combination of three sentences patterned after the four categorical sentence schemata. In short, we introduced fifteen valid *syllogistic* schemata. At the end of the section it was noted that there are valid arguments which are not patterned after any syllogistic schemata. We will refer to them as **nonsyllogistic arguments** and to their skeletons as **nonsyllogistic argument schemata.** Sometimes they involve categorical sentences, but frequently they do not. In this section we will examine the most important (useful) types of nonsyllogistic argument schemata.

Consider the following argument:

> *If* John is alone *then* Bob is alone.
> John is alone.
> So, Bob is alone.

The pattern of this argument is:

> If ___ then _ _ _.
> ___.
> So, _ _ _.

The words 'if' and 'then' in the first line tell us two things. First, they tell us that if the sentences following 'if' and 'then' are both true, then the *whole* sentence is true. For example, if

> John is alone.

and

> Bob is alone.

are both true, then the whole sentence

> If John is alone then Bob is alone.

is true. Second, they tell us that if the sentence following 'if' is true but the sentence following 'then' is false, then the *whole* sentence is false.

For example, if

John is alone

is true but

Bob is alone

is false, then the whole sentence

If John is alone then Bob is alone.

is false. It does not matter what *sentence* we put in place of the solid line following 'if' and the broken line following 'then'. The solid and broken lines are place markers for *any sentences* (including the trivial case in which the very same sentence is put in place of both the solid and the broken lines).
The

If ＿＿ then ＿ ＿ ＿.

form appears over and over in the study of logic. It is called a **conditional schema**. When the solid and broken lines are replaced by *sentences* (*not* just general terms), the result is a **conditional sentence**. A sentence following 'if' is called the **antecedent** of the conditional and a sentence following 'then' is called the **consequent**. Hence,

John is alone.

is an antecedent and

Bob is alone.

is a consequent. In different conditional sentences, the roles of these simple sentences might be completely reversed. The terms *antecedent* and *consequent* merely tell us where various sentences happen to be located in other sentences.
The argument schema

If ＿＿ then ＿ ＿ ＿.

＿＿.

So, ＿ ＿ ＿.

is as old as Barbara, and it has been given a number of names. In Latin it was called *modus ponendo ponens* which means the mood which affirms by affirming. This is a fairly descriptive name because anyone who uses an argument patterned after this schema begins with a conditional sentence, affirms its antecedent as a second premiss, and ends up detaching and affirming its consequent by itself. So, one *does* affirm by affirming with this pattern.

If someone begins with a conditional sentence, affirms its *consequent* as a second premiss and then detaches and affirms its antecedent all by itself, then he commits the (formal) **fallacy of affirming the consequent.** If we use the small letters '*p*', '*q*', and '*r*' as place markers for ordinary *sentences*, then we may write the valid **affirming mood** thus:

If *p* then *q*
p
Therefore, *q*

and the invalid fallacy of affirming the consequent so:

If *p* then *q*
q
Therefore, *p*.

It is possible to replace the place markers in this schema in such a way that its premisses are both true but its conclusion is false. For example,

If Ann is drawing a square then Ann
is drawing a polygon.
Ann is drawing a polygon.
Therefore, Ann is drawing a square.

The point is that both of the given premisses could be true although Ann is *not* drawing a square but, say, a trapezoid. Right? Unlike the affirming mood, this schema is not reliable. We can "feed it" only true premisses and it can still "crank out" false conclusions.

The mood which denies by denying (*modus tollendo tollens*) is similar to the affirming mood and at least as old. We will call it the **denying mood** for short. It is a valid schema which runs:

If *p* then *q*
Not *q*
So, not *p*.

Here we begin with a conditional sentence schema, deny its consequent as a second premiss and then detach and deny its antecedent. For example,

> If Ted is home then his coat must be here.
> But his coat is not here.
> So, Ted is not home.

Clearly, we end up denying *by* denying.

If someone begins with a conditional sentence, denies its antecedent as a second premiss and then detaches and denies its consequent all by itself, then he commits the (formal) **fallacy of denying the antecedent.** This fallacy runs:

> If *p* then *q*
> Not *p*
> So, not *q*

The following example shows that it is invalid:

> *If* Ann is drawing a square then Ann is
>   drawing a polygon.
> But Ann is not drawing a square.
> So, Ann is not drawing a polygon.

Ann *could* be drawing a polygon even though both of these premisses are true.

The following valid schema may remind you of Barbara:

> If *p* then *q*
> If *q* then *r*
> So, if *p* then *r*

We will call it **transitivity.** Here is an example patterned after transitivity:

> If Tom went home then Jerry went home.
> If Jerry went home then the party ended.
> So, if Tom went home then the party ended.

Notice that although transitivity may remind you of Barbara, it is not composed of categorical sentence schemata, and its place markers are definitely to be replaced by sentences rather than general terms.

The last valid argument schema we have to consider is called **constructive dilemma**. It runs:

> If p then q
> If r then s
> p or r
> Hence, q or s.

This looks complicated, but it is practically two *affirming moods* put together. That is, look at it this way:

> If p then q If r then s
> p or r
> So, q or   s.

An example of an argument patterned after the constructive dilemma is:

> If Helen talks then Harold is silent.
> If Carole talks then Clarke is silent.
> Either Helen or Carole will talk.
> Hence, either Harold or Clark will be silent.

Finally, it should be noted that the conditional schemata which we have been expressing as

$$\text{If } p \text{ then } q$$

could be expressed without 'then' thus:

$$p \text{ only if } q$$

and, by reversing the position of the antecedent and consequent, so:

> q if p
> q provided that p
> q in case p.

Hence, the affirming mood might be expressed in various ways, e.g.,

> q if p p only if q q in case p
> p p p
> So, q So, q So, q.

And, of course, similar switches may be made in the other schemata.

Review problems for Sec. 1.4

I. Explain the following:

1. antecedent
2. consequent
3. conditional sentence schema

II. Explain the difference between

1. the affirming mood and the fallacy of affirming the consequent
2. the denying mood and the fallacy of denying the antecedent

III. Indicate whether the following are patterned after:
   - (am)   affirming mood
   - (fac)   fallacy of affirming the consequent
   - (dm)   denying mood
   - (fda)   fallacy of denying the antecedent
   - (t)   transitivity
   - (cd)   constructive dilemma
   - (n)   none of these

1. The milkman is not wild if the general is honest. The general is not honest. Thus the milkman is wild.
2. A stitch in time is usually late provided that a boy scout is sick. A boy scout is sick. So, a stitch in time is usually late.
3. If Sally used Dial then she would have more friends. If she had more friends she would be happy. Therefore, she should use Dial.
4. In case you are interested, there is a snake in your closet. There must not be a snake in your closet. So, you must not be interested.
5. If Ed is dead then Red is dead. If Frank robbed the bank then Frank was tanked. Either Ed is dead or Frank robbed the bank. So, either Red is dead or Frank was tanked.
6. A boy must be neat only if he is not watched. If he is not watched then he will get drunk. So, a boy will get drunk provided that he must be neat.
7. Either Lola is simple or Frank is shrewd. Frank is not shrewd provided that he is drunk.
8. If I sent a horse to you for every time you made me blue, you would have a room full of horses. You have no horses in your room. I have not sent a horse to you for every time you made me blue.
9. That tree will lose its leaves if it is deciduous. That tree will lose its leaves. Thus, it must be deciduous.
10. The wire will conduct electricity provided that it is a copper wire. If the wire conducts electricity then Jones will be surprised. Therefore, in case it is a copper wire, Jones will be surprised.

11. If Belle is either sick or pretending then Sam must have been here. Sam has not been sick. So, Belle is neither sick no pretending.

12. A noneater will not starve if he keeps cool. But noneaters keep cool. So, noneaters will starve.

13. Roger is sick in case Suzie is unhappy. Bill is sick provided that Daphne is unhappy. Either Suzie or Daphne is unhappy. So, either Roger or Bill is sick.

14. If a bull is alone in the yard then a horse was eating hay. An ear of corn tastes good in case a horse was eating hay. Therefore, a bull is alone in the yard only if an ear of corn tastes good.

15. Either there is a thief in the room or someone is lying. Someone is lying. Thus, there is no thief in the room.

16. John ran for the bus provided that Elsie did not help Mary. Elsie did not help Mary. So, John ran for the bus.

17. A fool can win your heart only if you are a bigger fool. A fool cannot win your heart. Thus, you are not a bigger fool.

18. If the velocity is increased then the pressure will be decreased. The pressure is decreased only if the pump is broken. Thus, the pump is broken provided that the velocity is increased.

19. If the undulatory theory of light holds then light travels faster in air than in water. Light does travel faster in air than in water. Thus, the undulatory theory of light holds.

chapter
two BEGGING THE QUESTION

*The business of the educator is to see to
it that the greatest possible number of ideas
acquired by students are acquired in such
a vital way that they become moving ideas, motive-
forces in the guidance of conduct.* John Dewey

An argument may be unsound for three reasons. (1) It may be formally fallacious, i.e., have an invalid form. (2) It may have a false premiss, or (3) it may be irrelevant or circular. The latter mistakes are directly related to content (rather than form), so they are called 'informal fallacies'.

We examined two formal fallacies in the last chapter, namely the fallacy of affirming the consequent and the fallacy of denying the antecedent. In the remaining chapters we are going to concentrate on informal fallacies. The word 'fallacy' comes from the Latin *fallere* or *fallacia*, meaning to deceive or deception, respectively. As you will see shortly, many of the things we will call 'fallacies' are nothing more than *deceptions*. They may be intentional or unintentional, but they are nonetheless deceptive. From a moral point of view, it is extremely important to distinguish intentional from unintentional deceptions or fallacies. Indeed, from that point of view it might be useful to use the word 'deception' only for intentional errors, and 'fallacy' for unintentional ones. From a logical point of view, however, the distinction is unimportant because we are only concerned with the errors themselves, not with the character of the person committing them. Hopefully, by calling them to your attention and *naming* them we will be able to help you avoid them.

Many logicians have suggested different classifications of fallacies, and there is very little agreement about the number and kinds of sub-classes required for an exhaustive division. From the point of view of *neatness*, it is indeed unfortunate that no satisfactory classification has been designed. But from the practical point of view (i.e., insofar as one is concerned *primarily* with the recognition of fallacies) such a classification is *unnecessary*. A great deal of constructive work can be done without it. Hence, it should be noted that the division of fallacies presented here is at best plausible and convenient.

We seldom defend a view that we do not favor and we often assume that any view we favor is true. Hence, when we are constructing arguments in support of our views, it often happens that we simply *assume* the view we should be proving. When this happens, the fallacy of **begging the question** (*petitio principii*, i.e., assuming an inferior or less than self-evident principle) is committed. Question-begging arguments are *unsound* but *valid*, i.e., they do not involve any *formal* fallacy. They are unsound because in one way or another a question at issue is *assumed* rather than proved. Seven more or less subtle ways to commit this fallacy will be introduced.

2.1   Alleged certainty

One way to defend a view from attack is to present it as if it were *certain* or entirely beyond question. If a listener can be convinced immediately that what you are saying is true, you are spared the burden of constructing a genuine proof. Some claims, of course, are obviously true and it is surely no fallacy to say so. However, if a claim in question or doubt is qualified by a phrase which has the effect of persuading (without proving) that the claim is beyond doubt, then the fallacy of **alleged certainty** is committed. For example, consider the difference in the force of the following claims:

> The population of California is larger than
>   that of New York.
> Surely nobody would doubt that the population
>   of California is larger than that of New York.
> It would be silly to deny that the population of
>   California is larger than that of New York.
> Everyone knows that the population of California
>   is larger than that of New York.

The first of these claims has as much justification as the other three, but the other three *seem* more convincing. The other three are more *persuasive*. They tend to suppress our critical powers before the latter begin to operate. However, while the original claim may be true, it is not obviously so. Hence, the attempt to make it appear so must be considered a fallacy of *alleged certainty*.

2.2   Question-begging epithets

The fallacy of **question-begging epithets** is committed when, describing an issue, epithets are applied to it which not only *describe* it but *evaluate* it. Instead of introducing the issue in neutral or nonbiased terms, one introduces it using laudatory or vituperative epithets. Compare, for example, the following claims:

> Johnson introduced a new tax bill.
> Johnson introduced a long-awaited and extremely
>   needed tax bill.
> Johnson introduced another tax gimmick to
>   fill the government's pockets.
> Quick-draw Johnson unloaded another-get-rich-
>   quick tax bill.

In each of the last three claims an event is not only described but it is *evaluated*, and the evaluation is presented as if it were a simple statement of fact. This is the fallacy of *question-begging epithets*.

2.3   Circular reasoning

The fallacy of **circular reasoning** is committed whenever the conclusion one is trying to establish is either used as a premiss or presupposed by a premiss. For example, consider the following arguments.

> If God does not exist, men should not worship.
> But men should worship.
> _____
> God exists.

> If God does not exist, men should not believe
> everything that is written in the Bible.
> But men should believe everything that is
> written in the Bible.
> _____
> God exists.

> The Soul is simple because it is immortal, and
> it must be immortal because it is simple.

Since the conclusion of the first two examples is that God exists, the existence of God is evidently the question at issue. The second premiss of the first argument asserts that men should worship. But men should worship only if God exists, since men are not obliged to worship non-entities. Hence, if the truth of this premiss is granted, then the question at issue is answered in favor of God's existence. That is, the argument only "proves" the existence of God *after* that existence is *assumed*, i.e., it is circular.

Similar remarks apply to the second argument. Its second premiss is true only if God exists, since men are not obliged to believe falsehoods and *one* of the assertions in the Bible is that God exists. Thus, if the truth of this premiss is granted, then the question at issue is again answered in favor of God's existence, i.e., the argument is circular.

The third argument is the most obvious of the three. The soul's simplicity is supposed to follow from its alleged immortality, and the the latter is "proved" by appealing to the former. Hence, the simplicity of the soul is "proved" by this argument only *after* that simplicity is *assumed*, i.e., the argument is circular.

2.4 Question-begging definitions

The fallacy of **question-begging definitions** is committed when some essential words of a presumably factual but questionable assertion are defined in such a way that the assertion must be certain, but cannot be factual. Suppose, for example, it is claimed that all farmers are slow learners. Then a man who has been farming for *ten* years comes along who, according to all tests, would be considered a fast learner. Rather than admit a *counter* or *negative instance* to the generalization, we might define "farmers" as those who have been farming for *twenty* years. When a man who has been *dairy* farming for twenty years appears to be a fast learner, we claim that dairy farming is not "really" farming at all. Similarly, the fast-learning *mink* farmer is not a "real" farmer. Little by little it becomes clear that the generalization cannot possibly have a counterinstance because the key word "farmers" is being defined and redefined to meet all challenges. That is, all farmers are slow learners because anyone who learns fast is immediately excluded from the class of farmers. The truth of the questionable empirical assertion is guaranteed by the persistent *question-begging definition* of "farmers". Therefore, while the assertion must not be questionable, it cannot be empirical either.

Again, suppose it is claimed that a good halfback never moves in the direction of his own goal, i.e., he always runs towards his opponent's goal. Then it is pointed out that some halfbacks who are generally considered good often run away from their opponent's goal in order to insure longer gains. To save the generalization by a *question-begging definition*, we could claim that although these halfbacks are *considered* good, they are not "really" good. People who "really" understand football never even consider such halfbacks good, because, of course, whoever considers these halfbacks good, just doesn't understand football. And so it goes, facts cannot shake the generalization because its truth is guaranteed by definitions.

Similarly, it might be claimed that Italians love music, because anyone who does not love music is either not Italian at all or only partly so. Mathematical problems are neat, because messy problems are never "thoroughly" mathematical. Criminals cannot be rehabilitated, because anyone who can be rehabilitated is not a "genuine" criminal. In each of these cases, the truth of an allegedly empirical claim is guaranteed by the *question-begging definition* of the essential terms.

2.5 Complex questions

The fallacy of **complex** or **leading questions** is committed whenever a question is phrased so that it cannot be answered without granting a particular answer to some question at issue. For example, suppose the question at issue is whether or not Orville has *ever* gambled on Sundays? His mother-in-law raises the complex question: Are you still gambling on Sundays? Whether Orville answers Yes or No to this question, he has apparently admitted that he *has* gambled on Sundays, and that was the question at issue.

Again suppose the question at issue is whether Alice should take a train to New York or drive her father's car. Her father raises the complex question: Will you be taking the 8:40 or the 10:30 train? No matter which alternative Alice chooses, the question at issue has already been answered for her.

Finally, the question at issue is much too often whether one should fix the old car or buy a new one. And typically the automobile dealer begins with the question: What sort of car were you looking for? As far as he is concerned, the real question at issue has already been answered. But the truth of the matter is that he has simply committed the fallacy of *complex questions*.

2.6 *Assuming a more general claim*

The fallacy of begging the question by **assuming a more general claim** is committed when a principle which is more general and implies an answer to some question at issue is assumed. For example, suppose one is trying to prove that sociological laws are uncertain or unreliable. We may beg the question in his favor by *assuming the more general claim* that all knowledge about human beings is uncertain or that the behavior of human beings is "essentially" unpredictable. If the question is whether or not the United States should enter into an alliance with Yugoslavia, one might beg the question by *assuming the general principle* that no alliances with Communist nations should be formed. If the question is whether or not a student *deserves* to have his mark changed, an instructor might beg the question by *assuming the general principle* that marks never merit reconsideration.

2.7 *Assuming every instance of a generalization*

If the question at issue is a general claim or principle, the fallacy of begging the question by **assuming every instance of a generalization** may be committed by assuming the truth of every *instance* of it. Suppose, for example, the question is whether or not the United States should form an alliance with the countries behind the Iron Curtain. The question may be begged in favor of *not* forming such an alliance by assuming that the United States should not form an alliance with the Soviet Union, East Germany, Rumania, etc. That is, the *whole question may be begged in parts.*

Again, suppose the question is whether or not Negroes should be allowed to enter some school. The general question may be begged in parts if it is assumed that every Negro applicant is unacceptable. While the general question is prima facie left open, insofar as an assumption is made about each instance of it, the question is closed.

2.8   Equivalent expressions

The fallacy of begging the question with **equivalent expressions** is committed by assuming an answer in the form of an *equivalent* (but more or less unrecognizable) *expression*. For example, suppose a student magazine is printed and distributed in and around some college. One of the good citizens of the community decides that some of the stories and poems are shockingly filthy and blasphemous. He writes scathing letters to the president of the college, to the local paper, his state senator, his pastor, his mother, and many others. The president replies that he will look into the matter and that it is likely that the students involved were encouraged by some faculty malcontents. In a fairly roundabout fashion, the president has assumed the legitimacy of the critic's charges. Faculty *advisors* would be expected to encourage the publication of ordinary (acceptable) literature. Faculty *malcontents* would be expected to encourage the publication of *some* sort of unacceptable literature. Hence, by referring to the advisors as "malcontents", the president supported the charges of the community critic, i.e., he begged the question of guilt using an *equivalent* but somewhat disguised *expression*.

Fairly obvious cases of question-begging by *equivalent expressions* may result from converting or transposing sentences. For example, if the question at issue is

Are any cowboys millionaires?

it may be begged by assuming

Some millionaires are cowboys.

as a premiss. If the question at issue is

Are all Texans cowboys?

it may be begged by assuming

All non-cowboys are non-Texans.

as a premiss.

Review problems for Secs. 2.1–2.8

I.   Distinguish the following forms of question-begging:

1.   alleged certainty
2.   question-begging epithets
3.   circular reasoning
4.   question-begging definitions
5.   complex questions
6.   assuming a more general claim
7.   assuming every instance of a generalization
8.   equivalent expressions

II.   Name and explain the type of question-begging involved in each of the following:

1.   QUESTION: Must every player on the basketball team be over six feet tall?
     COACH: To begin with, we should grant that both forwards, the center, and both guards have to be over six feet tall.
2.   QUESTION: Are avid hunters more insensitive than philatelists?
     PACIFIST: Hunters are the most insensitive group of people in the world.
3.   QUESTION: Why are there juvenile delinquents?
     SOCIOLOGIST: There are juvenile delinquents because many juveniles break the law, and the reason so many juveniles break the law is that they are juvenile delinquents.
4.   As anyone in his right mind will tell you, all Sicilians carry knives.
5.   QUESTION: Did Fipps lie?
     PROSECUTOR: The story Fipps told was intentionally misleading.
6.   QUESTION: Is Zelda the designer of that house?
     CRITIC: There are no female architects.
7.   QUESTION: Can Sam be trusted?
     SAM: You mean can *old reliable* Sam be trusted?

8. Is Berford still sucking his thumb?
9. Everyone knows you can't trust a man who was born beside a leaky faucet.
10. QUESTION: How do you know that stranger is an outlaw?
    MAT: Cus' there ain't no other kind of stranger.
11. QUESTION: Are all the James boys outlaws?
    CHESTER: I couldn't say that, but Frank and Jesse are outlaws.
12. QUESTION: Is Willard a good soldier?
    CAPTAIN: Willard is the kind of man who runs when the enemy attacks.
13. QUESTION: Is the gift worth anything?
    SPEAKER: Colonel Crumb has honored our fair city by giving us his granddaddy's sword.
14. QUESTION: Did Klutz plan to murder Benz?
    PROSECUTOR: Mr. Klutz, what made you think your plan would work?
15. Certainly we need a new ball park if our children are going to be kept off the streets. If we need a new ball park then we must borrow money from New York. So because we must borrow money from New York, it follows that we need a new ball park.

III. Make up examples of each of the fallacies distinguished in Part I.

chapter
three   PSEUDOAUTHORITY

*If our civilization is to survive, we must
break with the habit of deference to great men. Great
men may make great mistakes.*   Karl R. Popper

Very early in our lives we are taught to respect authority. We learn to obey the rules of our parents, guardians, teachers, ministers, civil authorities, peer group organizations, etc. When you stop and think about the number of authoritative legislators we confront in a lifetime, it is a wonder that we are all not a little schizophrenic.

The fallacies introduced in this chapter take advantage of our conditioned response to marks of authority. They make the most of the peculiar devices that most people develop to move more or less freely in the midst of certain definite restrictions. Since each of the specific fallacies introduced here involves an appeal to some sort of illegitimate or pseudoauthority, we may refer to them collectively as fallacies of **pseudoauthority**. The traditional Latin name is *argumentum ad verecundiam*, i.e., literally, an argument to modesty. Each of the arguments presented makes an appeal to one's modesty in the face of some alleged authority. Each one is an *argumentum ad auctoritatem*, i.e., an argument or appeal to authority. They *may* all be committed without making any formal mistake, i.e., they are all *informal* fallacies.

3.1   Popular sentiments

The fallacy of appealing to **popular sentiments** (*argumentum ad populum*, i.e., to the people) is committed when, in the absence of a plausible argument for some view, the *feelings* or *attitudes* of a group of people are appealed to to win acceptance. Suppose, for example, that a prosecutor is unable to prove that a defendant is guilty of treason. In the absence of genuine evidence, he proceeds to point out the evils of treason. He reminds the jury that anyone who would aid or comfort an enemy of his own country ought to be severely punished; that anyone who would sell out his own people belongs behind bars; that treason is a sin against God and country; that a jury which would acquit such a man would surely face the judgment of their consciences. By skillfully tugging at the emotional heartstrings of the jury, by appealing to the *sentiments* of the people, the prosecutor may be able to get his view accepted.

Advertisers and salesmen often commit the fallacy of *popular sentiments*. One might even say with Willie Loman that "it comes with the territory". But what, after all, is the force of such arguments as the following?

> Our sewing machine is made in America by
> American engineers and technicians.
> _____
> Our sewing machine is well made

> I've been selling used cars on this corner
> for twenty years. My daddy sold
> cars on this corner, and my granddaddy
> sold buggies on this corner. My little
> boy (bless his heart) sells newspapers
> on this corner.
> _____
> I would not defile the great heritage of
> this corner by selling you a substandard
> automobile.

> Knowledge is power. The wise man is a wealthy
> man. He who faces the modern world without
> an education enters the battle of
> life unarmed. Any man who does not
> guarantee his child the finest education
> that money can buy has neglected
> his God-given duty.
> _____
> This encyclopedia I am selling is a bargain.

In the first case, the appeal is made to one's national patriotism, in the second, to one's local patriotism and general respect for longevity of business establishments, and finally, the appeal is made to the advantages of knowledge and the responsibilities of parenthood. These are appeals to *popular sentiments*.

3.2   Confident manner

The fallacy of deceiving people with a **confident manner** is committed when, in the absence of a legitimate argument, someone behaves as if he had a conclusive demonstration of his view. The fallacy may be illustrated by the preacher who scribbled the following note beside a paragraph in his sermon. "The argument is weak. Shout like mad!" No doubt you learned the trick years ago.

A pair of deuces backed up by a *confident manner* can be a strong poker hand. It depends on who is bluffing and who is supposed to be bluffed. Similarly, when you do not know the answer to a question, it is sometimes enough to *sound* as if the answer you do have is right. While bluffing often pays off in one way or another, from the logical point of view one who bluffs commits the fallacy of deceiving people with a *confident manner*.

3.3   Ceremony

The fallacy of *ceremony* is roughly an institutionalized form of the fallacy of *confident manner*. The fallacy of **ceremony** is committed when an indefensible view is supported by a peculiar ritual or setting. For example, if the wealthy Mr. Hogitall gives a large grant to a university in exchange for an honorary doctorate, the administrators of the university may have very little to say or do beyond committing the fallacy of *ceremony*. They can hardly announce at convocation that Hogitall bought himself the degree, but almost anything they say that would tend to make him *worthy* of the honor is a lie. So they all put on their dark robes; they march solemnly; the choir sings the alma mater and the boy scouts raise the flag. In short, the administrators commit the fallacy of *ceremony* by letting the ceremony do the lying for them.

Again, suppose a gas station owner is looking for a gimmick to increase business. He could give away a case of pop with every ten gallon purchase.

But pop is expensive. Alternatively he could string little flags all over his lot and put up a few huge signs, but *give away* only one bottle of pop. The gimmick now is not what he is giving away, but what he *seems* to be giving away. By changing the *setting* he has made his offer appear more valuable than it is. This is another instance of deception with *ceremony*.

3.4 Jargon

When a claim (or title, product, etc.) is made to appear stronger (or more important, valuable, etc.) than it is by the use of bombastic or technical-sounding language, the fallacy of appealing to the authority of **jargon** is committed. Suppose, for example, that you are offered a job as Assistant Service Director of Health, Sanitation, and Welfare. It sounds good, but it turns out to be the title of the number two man on a garbage collection truck. Here the fallacy of appealing to the authority of **jargon** has been committed by assigning a glamorous title to a pretty smelly job.

Nowadays, one is frequently taken in by the exotic names attached to synthetic materials. What is listed in the catalog as "sturdy neolast-forever plastic formula 231" turns out to be a cheap grade of plastic. The "rough, tough sterno-life polyfiberboard number 6" turns out to be some kind of cardboard. A fallacy is committed because instead of giving accurate descriptions (perhaps with some helpful *comparisons*) of a product, we are given technical terms which suggest a quite different product.

3.5 Aphorisms

The fallacy of appealing to the authority of **aphorisms** is committed when an aphorism, proverb, maxim, or cliché is used as a substitute for a good reason. We seem to have aphorisms to fit just any occasion, not to mention an innate capacity for formulating new ones. For example, consider the case of a student who was apprehended by the local police for necking with his girl in the backseat of an abandoned bus. When asked why he picked that place, he answered, "When Nature calls, one must respond". Instead of giving the real reason, he coined a new *cliché* and hoped for the best.

A football coach used the maxim "Never think: react!" to solve many of his problems. Whenever a player would try to explain why he was not where he should have been by pointing out that he *thought* such and such, out came the maxim. The maxim was a substitute for a good reason for *not* thinking. His proverbial ace in the hole was "People who make mistakes always make excuses". Even if one had a legitimate excuse, it was immediately undermined by this proverb. That is, the aphorism was used in place of a good reason for the coach's wholly unreasonable attitude toward anyone else's reasons for making mistakes! This sort of maneuver is typical of those who deceive others and/or themselves with aphorisms.

3.6   Popular people

The fallacy of appealing to the authority of **popular people** is committed when it is argued that a certain claim must be true because some well-known person believes it. This is often referred to as the *ipse dixit* fallacy i.e., *He* himself said it, therefore it is true, Now, the strength of a claim is not determined by the *name* of the person supporting it, but by the *evidence* one *has* adduced or *could* adduce. Hence, even if the well-known person is a recognized and reliable authority, his view is decisive only insofar as the evidence he produces or can produce is decisive; no further. Whatever the evidence fails to support, a popular name cannot support either.

In practice, the fallacy is usually committed in a fairly obvious fashion. Consider that vast number of movie stars and athletes that have been used to endorse everything from orange juice to airplanes. The advertiser never claims that the "star" is a recognized authority in the field, say, of citrus juices. It is not necessary. He knows that many people admire the "star" and that many will jump from 'the star is good' to 'the product is good'. And that is just the fallacious leap he is encouraging. Hence, both the advertiser (wittingly) and the consumer (unwittingly) commit the fallacy of appealing to the authority of *popular people*.

The fallacy is not eliminated by the *kind* of products or people involved. The arguments leading from

Star X believes it.

to either

You need Upforever Garters.

or

You should contribute to the Community Chest.

are equally fallacious. You might call this the 'good guy fallacy', i.e.,
Good guy X says that such and such is true, so it *is*.

3.7 Titles

The fallacy of appealing to the authority of **titles** is committed when it is
argued that a certain claim must be true because some significantly *titled*
people believe it. Consider the following examples.

Doctors believe Medicare is a mistake.
Medicare is a mistake.

Psychiatrists recommend pampering children.
Children should be pampered.

Senators say the war is just.
The war is just.

If it is a fallacy to appeal to the authority of some popular person's name,
it is *a fortiori* a fallacy to appeal to the authority of a *title* without naming
anyone in particular. While in the former case we are at least told exactly
who the authority is, in the latter case even that is withheld. In the latter
case there is not only a lack of evidence, but no clue is given for fixing the
responsibility to someone who could be expected to produce evidence.

3.8 Tradition

The fallacy of appealing to the authority of **tradition** or to the *wisdom of
the ages* is committed when it is argued that a claim must be true because
it has been traditionally supported or because it was supported in antiquity.
It is assumed, apparently, that what is old is good. But, as any antique
dealer will attest, a lot of old things are worthless.

The fallacy may be illustrated by the man who argued that people whose eyebrows come together are werewolves, because that had been said for years in his village. Surely, he claimed, our fathers and their fathers before them would not have imagined such a story themselves or passed it on without careful consideration. It never occurred to him that his relatives were as gullible as he.

Again, it has been argued that the ancients did not let their women have a voice in politics and that, therefore, women should not have a voice in politics today. If women had anything to contribute in the way of leadership, the ancients would have recognized it. The traditional role of women is the proper role because it is the traditional role! When the view is presented this way, the fallacy of *question-begging definitions* is also committed.

Finally, one must mention the argument that American negroes are inferior to other Americans because the former have traditionally been inferior to the latter. Negroes have traditionally held menial jobs and attended substandard schools. Therefore, they ought to hold menial jobs and attend substandard schools. They have traditionally been oppressed, so they ought to be oppressed. The fallacy of appealing to *tradition* could not be more poignantly illustrated.

Review problems for Secs. 3.1–3.8

I. Distinguish the following fallacies of pseudoauthority:

1. popular sentiments
2. confident manner
3. ceremony
4. jargon
5. aphorisms
6. popular people
7. titles
8. tradition

II. Name and explain the type of psuedoauthority appealed to in the following:

1. INSTRUCTOR: Describe the probable causes of the Thirty Years' War.
   STUDENT: I'm glad you asked that question. I spent all week getting ready for it. In fact, it's almost unfair to the other students to compare our essays. Anyhow, . . .

2. What do you mean, "Should we have turkey this Thanksgiving?" We've been eating turkey on Thanksgiving for thirty years.
3. POLITICIAN: Listen to me you *hicks*! I'm a hick just like you and that means I know what you got and what you ain't got.
4. ADVERTISEMENT: Modern science has found a way to keep those dentures in place. We call it "Stickalong 69".
5. PROFESSIONAL ATHLETE: I'd rather use Fudd's Mud than the greasy Kid Stuff.
6. QUESTION: Young man, why did you beat that innocent old lady to death? YOUNG MAN: Dem dat got it, get it and dem dat aint't got it, also get it. You dig?
7. ADVERTISER: Boy scouts always carry an extra bag of Bucko.
8. ADVERTISER: The first thing we'll do is hire a band. Then we'll rent a spotlight. We'll have seven girls dressed up like the seven dwarfs. If that doesn't bring 'em in, nothing will.
9. What do you mean, "Should we fight in Viet Nam?" You're an American aren't you?
10. HELP WANTED: Neat boy, 10–15, to be North-Central Area Dispatch Consultant and Field Representative for local newspaper.
11. Doctors and lawyers favor the bill.
12. If we ran a crooked business, your father and his father before him would have shopped somewhere else. But they both shopped here. What more could you ask?
13. Does it work? Man, I'm here to tell you that I will bet my right arm clean up to my left ear that this baby will pick up dirt that's only *thinking* about settling down on your rug.
14. QUESTION: Does it work?
    SALESMAN: You know what they say: You can be sure if it's Eastinglot.
15. COACH: If you want to be a champion, you have to look like a champion. Your clothes ought to look tailor-made. Your shoes should sparkle in the sunlight. When you do your calisthenics, you should make it look as if you were having a religious experience. That's how to be a champion.

III. Make up examples of each of the fallacies distinguished in Part I.

3.9 Large numbers

The fallacy of appealing to the authority of **large numbers** is committed when it is argued that a claim must be true because it is supported by many people. The supporters do not have to be popular or even hold important titles. The claim may not even be "tried and true". But if enough people are willing to stand up and be counted in support of a view, it begins to look plausible. It has been said, for instance, that fifty million Frenchmen can't be wrong. Although most people (hopefully) treat this as a trite and somewhat facetious saying, some do not.

With so many advertisers basing their "sales pitches" on the fact that *large numbers* of people bought their products in the past, it is likely that there are more than a few people who are persuaded by this fallacy. Most of us have seen arguments like the following:

> We sold more automobiles than anyone in
> town last year.
>
> You should buy an automobile from us.

> According to X's ratings, more people
> watch "Gunsmoke" than anything else.
>
> "Gunsmoke" is worth watching.

> More people smoke Cancerstick than any
> other cigarette.
>
> You will enjoy Cancerstick.

If these arguments were acceptable, we should have to grant that for a while the earth was flat, immobile, and at the center of the universe because *large numbers* of people believed just that. We should have to grant that the Mafia does not exist, since *large numbers* of people deny its existence. Clearly, the merit of a claim is not a simple function of the number of its supporters.

3.10 Self-interest

The fallacy of appealing to the authority of **self-interest** (*ad personam*) is committed when it is argued that a certain claim must be true because it is or could be especially beneficial to some particular person, namely *you*. It has often been referred to as an *appeal to the purse* (*argumentum ad crumenam*). It seems, unfortunately, that a man's interests are frequently interwoven so thoroughly with his purse strings that one may speak of the two things interchangeably, i.e., appealing to someone's *self*-interest is tantamount to appealing to his interest in his purse.

Suppose, for example, someone argued that the painting on your wall must be an original because an original would be more valuable than a copy. Again, he might argue that you should buy only originals because people will be more impressed with your good taste. Furthermore, he might point out that if you recommend him for a promotion, it is quite possible that he would be able to get you a good price on some originals. In fact because the price is likely to become proportionately lower as the recommendation gets better, it is obvious that he deserves an excellent recommendation. This is a perfectly straightforward appeal to *self-interest via the purse.* In reply to this appeal you might point out that you must be driving a new Chrysler instead of an old Ford because it is in your own best interests to be driving a Chrylser. And *you* must deserve a promotion because that's nice too, etc. While the appeal to *self-interest* provides a powerful psychological motive for believing that certain satisfying claims are true, it provides little else.

3.11   Irrelevant authority

The fallacy of appealing to **irrelevant authority** is committed when a reputable authority in one area is presented as an authority in an entirely different area. For example, one might argue that what Bertrand Russell has to say about religion is valuable because what he has said about mathematical logic is valuable. What the President has to say about foreign relations is reliable because what he has said about domestic relations is reliable.

We might be willing to accept, say, Russell's unproved claims about some issue related to mathematical logic, because in the past he has demonstrated competence in this area. His unsubstantiated claims in this area are like *promissory notes* with a very high cash value. It is highly probable that he can back up his claims here. But Russell's competence in religious matters, some would say, has not been demonstrated. In this area we do not know what his notes are worth. Hence, the appeal to Bertrand Russell as an authority on religion *because* he is an authority on mathematical logic is an appeal to an *irrelevant authority*.

3.12   Apriorism

The fallacy of **apriorism** is committed when it is argued *prior to any investigation* that certain events *must* occur or fail to occur because they are necessary according to some particular theory or view of the world. For example, someone might argue that nothing could convince him that there are ghosts because *he just knows* there are no ghosts. His claim is *not* that the concept of a ghost is incoherent or logically absurd, i.e., the term 'ghost' is not like the term 'square-circle'. Rather, he is claiming that he knows prior to investigation that there is nothing to be investigated. Instead of testing his views against the real world, he fashions or tries to fashion the real world according to his views.

A classic case of the *aprioristic* fallacy was the ancient philosopher Parmenides' "explanation" of change. Parmenides argued as follows:

(1) What is, exists.
(2) What is not, does not exist.
(3) So, nonbeing or the void does not exist.
(4) Hence, there is no empty place into which things might move.
(5) Thus, there is no motion.
(6) Therefore, since change involves *some* kind of motion, *nothing ever changes.*

A priori then, we know that things do not change. If we *seem* to perceive change, so much the worse for our perception!

Parmenides' argument rests on step (3) which seems to follow from step (2), but does not. Step (2) may be paraphrased

Whatever does not exist, does not exist.

which is trivially true and quite independent of any particular state of the world, i.e., it is not an empirical or factual claim at all. On the other hand, step (3) may be paraphrased

There is no empty space.

which is definitely an empirical claim and false. Following our senses, we might lead Parmenides to a rejection of his view by arguing that since *some* things change, there must be motion; and if there is motion, there must be empty space. According to the British philosopher Karl Popper, this was the approach used by the Greek philosopher Democritus.

3.13 Idols

The fallacy of appealing to the authority of **idols** is committed when the views of an individual are presented as those of a more or less mysterious and generally respected entity *or* group. For example, a lawyer might claim that if we attack his view, we are challenging the very principle of *Law*. We cannot then, reject his view without supporting anarchy. A teacher might argue that to challenge his authority in the classroom is to challenge *Authority*, and since *some* authority is necessary to keep social systems functioning, he must not be challenged. A minister might take the view that when he speaks, *The Church* speaks. A physician might argue that in attacking him we attack *the whole Medical Profession*.

Although some issues might be construed as involving basic principles and whole groups of individuals, it is a mistake to assume that this is true of all of them, e.g., we might very well criticize a negligent mother without attacking motherhood. Indeed, the negligent mother may be criticized in behalf of or in the name of the rights and duties of motherhood. When we challenge the crank scientist or the quack doctor, we are not attacking science and medicine. The very point of the attack is to strengthen the professions by eliminating the cranks and quacks.

3.14   Faith

The fallacy of appealing to the authority of **faith** is committed when it is insisted that the views for which some evidence might be adduced must be taken on *faith alone*. For example, suppose a man comes to your door selling vacuum cleaners. Unconvinced by his propaganda, you ask for a demonstration. He replies that he considers your request an insult, that you have no right to question his integrity or his product, that you ought to have faith in your fellowman. This is a fallacious appeal to *faith* because evidence for or against his claims could easily be produced.

Again, a painter might suggest that there is no need to give you a written estimate of costs before painting your house. After all, you should have *some faith* in your employees. But such faith is *unnecessary*. There are laws to protect people against thieves, and there is no need to take on faith what may be guaranteed by law.

Some issues, perhaps, cannot be settled without a "leap of faith". The so-called Great Issues of God, freedom and immortality, may be in this class. But there are plenty of not-so-great issues which are amenable to empirical investigation as well as logical analysis. The fallacy of appealing to *faith* is committed if such issues are settled by appealing to blind faith as a substitute for thorough research.

3.15 Misrepresenting authority

The fallacy of **misrepresenting authority** is committed if the claims of some reputable authority are substantially changed or completely fabricated. The meaning of a sentence might be *changed* by lifting it out of context, changing some of its terms, or emphasizing originally inessential parts. For example, suppose the following paragraph is attributed to some highly respected authority on political science:

> All systems of government are experiments.
> Democracy is an experiment. Communism is
> an experiment. *A priori* we do not know
> what form of government is best for a given
> society. Ordinarily we should encourage
> experimentation, but the possible
> cost of some experiments make them impractical.
> So it is with communism.

The fallacy of *misrepresenting authority* is committed if this paragraph is allegedly summarized by any of the following:

> Communism is an experiment and we should
> encourage experimentation.
> The possible costs of some experiments
> makes them impractical, but is it so with
> communism?
> *A priori* we do not know what form of government
> is best for a given society.
> Communism is just another experiment
> which should be encouraged.

Again, a university professor once suggested that it might be a good idea to have advocates of free love, atheism, communism, and fascism give lectures at the university. He thought it might be fairer to all, as well as more exciting, to allow his students to hear "the other side" directly. Denny Dimwit committed the fallacy of *misrepresenting authority* by reporting that his professor advocated free love, atheism, communism, and fascism. If the professor had suggested having a happy pregnant woman address the class on pregnancy, perhaps Denny would have caught on.

The fallacy might be committed by completely *fabricating* the claim of some authority. For example, if a speaker knows that his audience respects Daniel Webster, Saint Paul, or Calvin Coolidge, he might make up *anything* and attribute it to the proper authority. It is improbable that anyone memorized *every* word someone else wrote, so it is not likely that such fabrication would be challenged. Furthermore, the speaker might block serious repercussions by prefacing his lies with, "As Daniel Webster would have said . . ." or "As Daniel Webster is reported to have said . . ." In either case, the speaker has not claimed that Webster actually *did* say anything.

3.16 Imaginary authority

The fallacy of appealing to **imaginary authority** is committed when a purely fictional authority is introduced in support of some claim. For example, if a police investigator firmly believes that the suspect he is questioning is guilty, he might try to convince him that it is useless to withhold his confession because conclusive evidence has already been gathered. He may point to the file containing the *imaginary* evidence or refer to the *fictional* eyewitness in the other room. The guilty suspect might point out that he knows six *imaginary* people who will swear that he was at the opera at the time of the crime. Similarly, a scientist might appeal to the results of an *imaginary* experiment he allegedly performed. A psychiatrist might quote from *imaginary* clients. A historian might invent some important documents to vindicate his thesis, etc. Once one is committed to this sort of tactic (i.e., to telling lies), the possibilities are practically unlimited.

Review problems for Secs. 3.9–3.16

I. Distinguish the following fallacies of pseudoauthority:

1. large numbers
2. self-interest
3. irrelevant authority
4. apriorism
5. idols
6. faith
7. misrepresenting authority
8. imaginary suthority

II.   Name and explain the type of pseudoauthority appealed to in the following:

1.   SPEAKER: In the words of the great American George Washington, "Buy bonds".

2.   CRANK: Have I *tested* it? What is there to test? *I* made it up, didn't I?

3.   According to the Right Reverend Rand, Zeke doesn't have polio and that's good enough for me.

4.   Almost everyone in Milwaukee drinks it. What better recommendation could anyone offer?

5.   QUACK: Does it work? I had a patient in here just the other day, named Jones or Smith, or whatever it was, who took two swigs and *zingo* no more pain!

6.   QUACK: Boy, I can't cure your ills all by myself. You've got to *believe* in me and my methods. You've got to have confidence in my medicine. You've got to *believe*!

7.   I wouldn't say we sell the best concrete in the world, but I *would* say that if a man got a whole town to pave its roads with it, he would surely be well rewarded.

8.   If you miss *this* film you must have something against the whole movie industry.

9.   BRUTUS: I heard Mark Antony say he came to praise Caesar not to bury him.

10.   My uncle Ralfe, the barber, says it's easy to have babies, and that women who cry and moan during delivery are just chicken.

11.   TYRANT: If you oppose me you oppose Government.

12.   MECHANIC: Oh, it won't take much to fix that; a little time, a few dollars and it will be just like new. You don't need an estimate. Just trust me.

13.   BIGOT: He's a Greek, isn't he? That's all I need to know. I don't trust him.

14.   DRIVER: If *that* lane is open then how come all the cars are lined up in this one? That one must be closed.

15.   SENATOR, waving a blank sheet of paper: I have here the sworn testimony of four people!

III.   Make up examples of each of the fallacies distinguished in Part I.

IV.   The following questions are designed to review *all* of the fallacies discussed in Chapters 2 and 3. Name and explain the type of question-begging *or* pseudoauthority involved in each case:

1.   I don't see how you can call yourself a Texan and not contribute to the Save the Alamo Fund.

2.   I don't care what you saw. According to my calculations, it couldn't happen.

3.   JOHN: Sure he's a sailor. But how do you know he gambles?
EMMA: Because as far as I'm concerned there are no nongambling sailors.

4.   All I know is that's the way it has always been, and that's reason enough to accept it

5.   HONEY: What makes you think we have to buy a new radio?
SAM: Because we have to listen to more spy stories?
HONEY: Why do we have to listen to more spy stories?
SAM: Because we have to buy a new radio.

6. QUESTION: Are all of the Great Lakes polluted?
   SENATOR: Maybe not, but we assume Superior, Michigan, Huron, Erie, and Ontario are polluted.

7. Does the town need it? Baby, it will mean ten thousand dollars to you personally. Doesn't that answer your question?

8. MOVIE STAR: I think Crunchies are the greatest.

9. QUESTION: Are all Cubans farmers?
   STUDENT: To answer this question, let us assume merely that no Cubans are nonfarmers.

10. It's as plain as the nose on Durante's face that nobody could be allergic to dogs.

11. If you're going to buy an automobile here, you'll just have to trust me. There's no other way to be sure you're not getting a lemon.

12. I'll swagger in there with my head up and my muscles flexed. No one will bother me.

13. QUESTION: Is the university going to offer a course in drama?
    DEAN: That's an open question. All I know is that no fine arts courses will be introduced.

14. Who cares who said it. Tell them Elvis Fink said it two nights ago. They won't check it out.

15. That guy is the number one man in Egyptology in the country. If he says the Danes practiced animism, he ought to know.

16. ADVERTISEMENT: At last it's here. New polygrip neverslip multigrip adhesive 44.

17. QUESTION: Do we need a new fishing ordinance?
    SENATOR: Gentlemen, I would like to introduce a bill that is long overdue and eagerly awaited by most of the people in this community. It's a new fishing ordinance.

18. CAPTAIN: In the immortal words of John Paul Jones, I'd rather fight than switch.

19. JUDGE: Why did you kill Clarence?
    KILLER: You know what they say: There's a little good in the worst of us and a little evil in the best of us.

20. Everyone in town bought one last year. It must be good.

21. GENERAL: I don't know what to say either. I think it took more stupidity than courage. Let's give him a medal and let people draw their own conclusions.

22. QUESTION: Did Pablo poison Prudence?
    PROSECUTOR: Pablo, how long after you poisoned Prudence did you wait to call the police?

23. Judges recommend it highly.

24. GOVERNOR: You can't challenge me without challenging Government.

25. CANDIDATE: Nobody understands a Southerner like a Southerner, and I'm here to tell you good people that my heart belongs to Dixie just like yours.

chapter
four   IRRELEVANT
APPEALS

*You ought not to discuss with everybody or exercise
yourself against any casual person: for against
some people argument is sure to deteriorate . . .
and this can only result in a debased kind
of discussion.*   Aristotle

One of the fallacies identified earliest by the Greek philosopher Aristotle
was that of being ignorant of the question at issue (*ignoratio elenchi*, lit.
ignorant refutations). A fallacy of **ignoratio elenchi** is committed when
the *wrong point is proven* or when the conclusion established by some set of
premises is *irrelevant* to the point at issue. This chapter has been entitled
"Irrelevant Appeals" because in one way or another every instance of
ignoratio elenchi turns out to be just that—an irrelevant appeal. None of the
appeals presented has to involve a formal mistake, i.e., they are *informal*
fallacies.

There are as many types of *ignoratio elenchi* as there are irrelevant appeals
or irrelevant points to be proven. Indeed, even if our list of twenty-three
irrelevant appeals were expanded by adding the last sixteen appeals to
pseudoauthorities (a move one could easily justify), only a small sample
of the total number of such appeals would be presented.

4.1   Force

The fallacy of making an irrelevant appeal to **force** (*argumentum ad
baculum*) is committed when some kind of *force* or violence is used to bring

about the acceptance of some view. Examples with which you are probably familiar include the following:

> If I stepped out of bounds then I will
>   take my ball and go home.
> _____
> I did not step out of bounds.

> Either I'm right or you don't get the car tonight.
> _____
> I'm right.

> If it's your move I'll quit.
> _____
> It's my move.

In each of these cases, if the premisses prove anything, it is that some kind of *force* is going to be applied *unless* a certain view is accepted. Or, to put it in a slightly different way, a certain view is going to be accepted *or else*. But the threat of *force* or violence is beside the point. The question at issue, say, in the last example is *not* what happens if it's your move, but whose move it is. The appeal to *force* is, from a logical point of view, an irrelevant (though often persuasive) appeal.

4.2 Pity

The fallacy of introducing an irrelevant appeal to **pity** (*argumentum ad misericordiam*) is committed when one tries to persuade someone to accept a particular view by arousing his sympathy or compassion. For example, a defence attorney might try to persuade a jury that his client is innocent by listing *ad nauseum* the unfortunate consequences of a conviction. He might say that the client's wife would have to find a job and, being a dumb, sexy-looking woman, she would probably become a prostitute; the three children would be on the streets more often without anyone to watch them; no doubt the boy who has homosexual tendencies would become an overt homosexual; and so on. In view of all these "facts" the attorney would argue that his client must be innocent. The appeal is tear-jerking, but irrelevant.

Again, a student who missed practically every class and did nothing outside class to master the material told me that if he failed the course he would probably be drafted into the army. Other students have been faced with losing their parents' support, being thrown out of school, losing their girls or their fraternity membership. Even *after* the appeal to *pity* is explained to them, they come up with these howlers! But, of course, the question at issue in such cases is not what happens if the student fails, but whether or not he deserves to fail. The appeals to one's compassion are stimulating, but irrelevant.

4.3 Ignorance

The fallacy of appealing to **ignorance** (*argumentum ad ignorantiam*) is committed when it is argued that the absence of evidence for (against) a claim *must* be counted as evidence (for) it. For example, the failure to produce reliable evidence for (against) the existence of God might be used as evidence of His nonexistence (existence). The failure to disprove the existence of telepathy might be used as evidence for its existence. The failure of a person to think of a *better* course of action might be used as evidence that the present course is good. (They might all be bad.)

Now, usually one who makes an assertion must assume the responsibility of defending it. If this responsibility or *burden of proof* is shifted to a critic, the fallacy of appealing to *ignorance* is committed. Suppose, for example, that Tillie claims it is impractical to send a man to Mars because the money that will be required for the project could be spent on urgently needed artificial kidneys. Billy claims that the trip to Mars is *not* impractical. When Tillie asks Billy for a reason for his view, Billy replies, "Prove that I'm wrong". Billy has passed the burden of proof back to Tillie. Tillie has already defended her claim and now Billy is requiring her to defend *his* claim by an *argumentum ad ignorantiam*, i.e., *his* claim is supposed to be true provided that Tillie is unable to refute it.

Sometimes the failure to produce evidence *for* a claim *should* be counted as evidence *against* it. For example, suppose someone says there is an elephant in your room. If you go to your room, look all around, and fail to find any evidence in support of this claim, you are justified in treating this lack of *supporting* evidence as *disconfirming* evidence, i.e., the failure to find evidence for the claim may be considered evidence for the *denial* of the claim. Such a move is justifiable because a person can hardly fail to find evidence for the fact that an elephant is in his room *provided that* (1) he looks for it and (2) it is there. Hence, the failure to find evidence that an elephant is there must be counted as evidence that *no* elephant is there.

On the other hand, if someone claims that your room is full of air, the situation is quite different. Your room *is* full of air, but if you look around (i.e., as you might look around to find an elephant), you will not find any. Air is not the kind of thing you can find by just looking around. Hence, the fallacy of appealing to *ignorance* would be committed if someone argued that because the air cannot be seen, it must not exist. In short then, the failure to find evidence for a claim should be counted as evidence against it *provided that* such evidence is ordinarily observable when it exists. If the evidence is ordinarily unobservable when it exists, then the failure to observe it cannot prove anything.

4.4 Abusing the man

The fallacy of **abusing the man** (*argumentum ad hominem*) is committed when the defender of an issue is attacked instead of the issue itself. Suppose, for example, the only eyewitness to some crime happens to be an exconvict. Instead of denying the witness's testimony directly, the defense attorney tries to discredit it by discrediting its source, namely the witness. He informs the jury that people who have been in prison have very little respect for such things as truth, justice, or the law; that about two-thirds of all exconvicts return to prison; that it is much easier to lie than it is to commit almost any crime and that, therefore, the likelihood that an exconvict is a liar is very high, etc. In short, the argument of the defense attorney comes down to this:

> Exconvicts are bad men.
> ―――――――――――――――――
> Whatever they say is false.

The argument is equally fallacious if the bad man happens to be a Communist, slum landlord, sex pervert, etc. The evil that men do does not always affect their assertions.

Again, the fallacy of *abusing the man* might be committed by pointing out that a man's behavior is inconsistent with his claims, e.g.,

> He does not practice what he preaches.
> ―――――――――――――――――――――
> What he preaches is false.

> You would not want your sister to marry
> a Negro.
> ―――――――――――――――――――――
> Negroes are not as good as Caucasians.

In reply to the first argument it might be noted that although it is true that a person ought to do good rather than evil, most people talk about it much more than they practice it. In reply to the second argument, it might be remarked that you would not want your sister to marry your *brother* (or your father or mother for that matter), but that does not prove that your brother is not as good as your sister.

4.5   Bad Seed

The fallacy of the **bad seed** is committed when it is argued that the views of some descendant of a bad man must be false. Briefly, it comes down to this:

> He is a son of a bad man.
> ―――――――――――――――
> What he says must be false.

While the fallacy is a species of *abusing the man*, it contains a peculiar blunder of its own. Here it is assumed that a man's character, politics, or generally nefarious habits are passed on to his descendants, in his *seed* as it were. Hence, for example, the sons and daughters of former or current members of the Nazi party are saddled with the guilt of their fathers. Then, insofar as it is alleged to be impossible to get truth out of the latter, it is supposed to be impossible to get the truth out of the former. However, if it is a mistake to infer the falsehood of a claim from its *source, a fortiori* it is a mistake to infer the falsehood of a claim from some *offspring* of that source.

4.6   Bad connections

The fallacy of appealing to **bad connections** is committed when it is argued that the views of some person must be false because he has certain nefarious, unsavory, or *evil connections*. Clearly, this is a species of the fallacy of *abusing the man*. It might be illustrated thus:

> He has bad connections.
> ―――――――――――――――
> What he says must be false.

The *connections* might, of course, be hereditary; he might be a son of a bad man. In that case this fallacious appeal would be indistinguishable from the *bad seed* fallacy. On the other hand, he might just be familiar with criminals, oddballs, beatnicks, barflies or beach bums. Somehow the evil that a man's friends or acquaintances do is supposed to rub off on him and turn his truth claims into falsehoods. If this were true then social workers, priests, and "good Samaritans" would not only be corrupt (or corrupted sooner or later) but their assertions would have to be false.

4.7 Faulty motives

The fallacy of appealing to **faulty motives** is committed when it is argued that because someone's *motives* for defending an issue are not proper, the issue itself is unacceptable. Suppose, for instance, that the owner of the only lumber company in town proposes the construction of a wooden fence around the Little League ballpark. In reply to his suggestion, the city fathers argue that he is obviously only feathering his own nest and that, *therefore*, the ballpark does not need a fence. The fallacy of appealing to *faulty motives* has been committed because the truth or falsity of the lumberman's proposal cannot be inferred from his *motives*.

Again, the voters of a small town in New York voted down the construction of a new high school because it was proposed by the school authorities, namely the principal, staff, and P.T.A. It was claimed that because these people had a vested interest, a school was not needed. Hence, instead of considering the *evidence* presented by the school authorities, the voters considered likely *motives* and came to the conclusion that a new high school was not necessary.

4.8 You're another

The **you're another** (*tu quoque*) fallacy is committed when a person's inconsistent position with respect to some issue is used as an argument against it. In our discussion of *abusing the man* it was noted that the failure of a person's practices to agree with his principles might be fallaciously used against him. Sometimes *this* is referred to as the *tu quoque* fallacy. Here we have reserved the name *tu quoque* for the slightly but significantly different cases in which a man's behavior is perfectly consistent with his principles, but his *principles change* from time to time.

For example, people have claimed that President Johnson's view on integration must be false because earlier in his career he had a completely opposite view. Johnson's critics and opponents of integration argued that *even he* opposed integration a few years ago. Hence, their argument boils down to the claim that whatever view a man starts with is true, and he is stuck with it forever. There is no such thing as adopting a new, incompatible and perhaps better view of an issue. New and incompatible views are *ipso facto* unacceptable views according to those who employ the *tu quoque* fallacy.

Again, suppose the legislature of some state is considering the construction of a new superhighway. Those who favor it most strongly happen to be the very people who opposed it thirty years ago. The current opponents of construction use the inconsistency of the proponents' views as an argument against construction. To the current proponents they protest, "You opposed construction too! What you now propose is inconsistent with your original view. Therefore, what you now propose is unacceptable". This is the "you're another" or *tu quoque* fallacy.

Review problems for Secs. 4.1–4.8

I. Distinguish the following types of irrelevant appeals:

1. force
2. pity
3. ignorance
4. abusing the man
5. bad seed
6. bad connections
7. faulty motives
8. you're another

II. Name and explain the type of irrelevant appeal involved in the following:

1. What he says can't be true. After all, he hangs around with that bully on the next block.
2. What he says can't be true because he said just the opposite three weeks ago.
3. How do I know I'm right? Because no one has ever proved I'm wrong.
4. LAWYER: He must be lying. He's a two-time loser, isn't he?
5. Maybe you would like me to knock your block off to convince you that you need protection.

6. SPEEDER: Officer, if I don't get to work on time I'll lose my job. You *can't* stop me now.
7. He's a McCoy, and if that don't make him a no-good liar, what does?
8. The English support United States' policies in the Far East because they have to. So if an Englishman says any of their policies are good, don't believe him.
9. Every time I talk to you, you change your tune. You must be mistaken.
10. If there really was a good fairy, someone would have proved it by now. But nobody has even begun to prove it; so that just proves there isn't one.
11. He *couldn't* have spent the last eight years in the service and still be an honest man.
12. If the army is so great, why aren't you in it?
13. DEFENSE: Are you going to believe that this poor, ignorant, sickly, lonely, dirty, bewildered, frightened little girl could have planned to murder anyone?
14. GESTAPO: I can't force you to remember. But I wonder if you know how an animal feels when it's being branded.
15. Why should anyone believe an insurance salesman? They make their living selling insurance whether anyone needs it or not.

III. Make up examples of each of the fallacies distinguished in Part I.

4.9 Friendship

The fallacy of appealing to **friendship** (*argumentum ad amicitiam*) is committed when it is argued that a certain view must be acceptable because it is that of a friend.

> I'm your friend.
> _____
> What I say is true.

No doubt most of us allow ourselves to be taken in by this apparent fallacy much more frequently that we would care to admit. It is difficult to criticize a friend and, often enough, it is difficult to challenge his views without having the challenge interpreted as some kind of criticism. So we more or less unwittingly spare ourselves the unpleasantness of disagreement by letting gross exaggerations, strange descriptions, and peculiar value judgments pass without comment. We grant, for instance, that Charlie, whom our friend hates but we can find no good reason to hate, *should* be hated. We compliment Susie for her beautiful new dress which we believe looks terrible. After all, she's a *friend.* Why hurt her feelings? Maybe her dress really is beautiful. Okay, her dress *is* beautiful!

Clearly, the mere fact that a view is supported by or favorable to a friend does not prove that the view is acceptable. Certainly, a friend who insists on your agreement in the name of friendship is not much of a friend. But anyone who repeatedly accepts falsehoods in the name of friendship is not much of a friend either, though he might be a great therapist.

4.10   Fear

The fallacy of appealing to **fear** (*argumentum ad metum*) is committed when *fear* is used to persuade someone to accept some view. While it might be granted that whenever someone appeals to *force* he appeals to *fear*, it frequently happens that people appeal to *fear without* appealing to force. Hence, the two fallacies may be profitably distinguished. Consider a few examples of the fallacy of appealing to *fear*.

An insurance salesman drops in to "inform" you of the advantages of buying a policy and, incidentally, of the possible disadvantages of not buying one. He describes the plight of Benny Moreali on the other side of town whose house burned down. Benny kept all his money in a heavy oak chest, which, naturally, was completely destroyed. Benny's wife had always worked to make ends meet, but now his oldest son had to drop out of school to help carry the financial burden. Benny's new car (which also lacked insurance) was demolished when the burning house fell on it. Without ever appealing to *force*, the salesman is trying to drive you by *fear* to the conclusion that you need a policy. However, although the appeal to the fact that Benny's bundle burned might be persuasive, it is irrelevant to your own insurance needs.

Again, service station attendants on toll roads seem to have a penchant for appealing to fear. If a hose looks a little worn, they are prepared with a lecture on the evils of broken hoses. They say that if a hose bursts while you are out on the road, you will lose all your antifreeze and your block might crack from overheating. Dirty oil or oil filters lead to low mileage and greater expenses in the long run. How dirty should they get? Well, they are dirty enough to change right now. And that filthy money-wasting air filter! That should be changed. Have you had the car tuned lately? When it's not tuned properly, it just burns much more gasoline than necessary. A lot of hard-earned money goes down the drain. In all of these suggestions there is very little emphasis on the *evidence* substantiating the claim that *your* car needs attention, but a great deal of effort is expended trying to *frighten* you into spending a little more cash. This is a typical strategy for those who make irrelevant appeals to *fear*.

4.11 Wrong reason

If someone attacks some claim on the ground that it leads to contradictions, but in fact it is some *other* claim which is faulty, the fallacy of appealing to the **wrong reason** is committed. In Latin this is known as the fallacy of *non propter hoc*, lit., not because of *it*. As we have just suggested, this fallacy occurs in the context of a *reductio ad absurdum* type of argument. Someone attempts to prove that a claim is unacceptable because it leads to contradictions. He lists a set of premisses including the dubious claim and derives a contradiction. The fallacy of *wrong reason* is committed if a contradiction may be inferred from the set of premisses *without* the dubious claim.

Suppose someone presents the following argument:

(1) If Leavitt communicates with the spirits of the departed then he deserves a promotion.

(2) He does not deserve a promotion, but he does communicate with the spirits of the departed.

(3) Leavit has extrasensory perception.

Leavit deserves a promotion.

To prove that premiss 3 is false, an objector derives a contradiction from *all three* premisses. But a contradiction may be derived from the first two premisses alone, namely the following:

Leavitt deserves a promotion and does
not deserve a promotion.

Hence, the objector has committed the fallacy of *wrong reason*, i.e., premiss 3 has been rejected for the *wrong reason*.

Again, suppose the following argument is presented:

(1) Some lovers are not fighters.

(2) All soldiers are fighters.

(3) All lovers are soldiers.

(4) All soldiers are courageous.

(C) All lovers are fighters.

An objector claims that since the four premisses taken together lead to both (C) and its denial

Some lovers are not fighters.

premiss 4 must be rejected. However, the same contradiction may be derived from the first three premisses alone. Hence, premiss 4 has been rejected for the *wrong reason*.

4.12   Wishful thinking

The fallacy of **wishful thinking** is committed when it is claimed that something *is* the case because it *ought* to be, i.e., whatever is morally proper, *exists*. For example,

> Negroes ought to be able to vote without
>   being intimidated.
> _____
> They are able to vote without being intimidated.

> Americans ought to be loved by foreigners.
> _____
> They *are* loved by foreigners.

> The summer monsoon rains *ought* to be heavy
>   enough to sustain a good crop.
> _____
> The rains *will* be heavy enough.

Clearly, all our moral problems would be solved if things *were* exactly as they *ought* to be.

4.13   Is–ought

The **is-ought** fallacy is committed when it is claimed that what *is* the case, *ought* to be the case, i.e., whatever *exists*, is morally proper. For example,

> Every country *is* run by a small handful of
>   powerful people.
> _____
> Every country *ought* to be run by a small
>   handful of powerful people.

> Very few teachers join labor unions.
> Very few teachers *ought* to join unions.

If these arguments were acceptable, then the following would be acceptable too:

> The Nazis killed six million Jews.
> The Nazis *ought* to have killed six million Jews.
>
> Sixty percent of all burglaries *are* committed
>   by people under sixteen years of age.
> Sixty percent of all burglaries *ought* to
>   be committed by people under sixteen.

None of these arguments is acceptable.

4.14   Attacking illustrations

The fallacy of **attacking illustrations** is committed when a mere illustration or example of a point at issue is challenged instead of the point itself. For example, consider the case of a student and an instructor discussing the psychiatrist C. G. Jung's theory of "archetypes". According to the theory, people are supposed to have some more or less common *patterns* of thinking. To illustrate this (admittedly oversimplified) theory, the student suggests that the pattern might be *like* syllogisms. But the instructor objects that because some arguments are not syllogisms and some people never use syllogisms, the theory of "archetypes" must be false. The instructor has committed the fallacy of *attacking illustrations.* Syllogisms were suggested to illustrate the idea of a *pattern*, but the instructor treated the illustration as if it was the theory itself, i.e., as if Jung's theory proposed that all people use syllogisms.

   Again, imagine Slipanfall Smith asserting that it is possible to construct an apparatus that would enable a man to fly. Thomas, who does not understand exactly what Slipanfall has in mind, asks for an illustration. So Slipanfall makes a set of wax wings, straps them on his arms and leaps off the top of the nearest mountain. When he comes to, he hears Thomas saying, "There, you see? You were wrong. It is not possible to construct such an apparatus". Thomas has committed the fallacy of *attacking illustrations.* Slipanfall's claim was true, but his illustration was poor. The former cannot be falsified by the failure of the latter.

Review problems for Secs. 4.9–4.14

I. Distinguish the following types of irrelevant appeals:

1. friendship
2. fear
3. wrong reason
4. wishful thinking
5. is-ought
6. attacking illustrations

II. Name and explain the type of irrelevant appeal involved in the following:

1. If you were really my friend you would not doubt my word.
2. The best argument against the claim that we ought to have a democracy is the simple fact that we do not have one.
3. SPEAKER: The wheel continues to turn by the force of the water in much the same way that a wheel may be kept in motion by a small mouse walking inside it.

    HECKLER: And how much electricity are we supposed to get from one mouse?
4. Well, if you don't mind losing a tire, going off the road, and maybe killing yourself, you don't need a new tire.
5. MAYOR: In the first place, everyone knows we need a fire engine. In the second place, we need a new ambulance. And finally, at least one person thinks we do not need a new fire engine.

    ALDERMAN: If we accept those points we're committed to nonsense. Clearly, we don't need an ambulance.
6. He won't die, because he's a good man, and good men should live a lot longer than he has lived.
7. INSTRUCTOR: Suppose, for example, that there were only two people in the world. According to Hobbes, they would naturally want to destroy each other.

    STUDENT: The theory is silly because there will never be only two people in the world.
8. You can sell your house to anyone, but don't expect the boys at the club to stand by you and don't think you're not going to lose customers.
9. Of course it's your house. But I'm your buddy and I say you can't sell to those people.
10. I know he should be here at eight, and as far as I'm concerned, that means he will be.

11. He's in jail, isn't he? Then that's just where he belongs.

III. Make up examples of each of the fallacies distinguished in Part I.

4.15   Straw man

The fallacy of attacking a **straw man** is committed when a weak *argument* for a view or an *implausible* statement of a view is attacked (usually successfully) instead of equally accessible stronger arguments or more plausible statements.

Consider the following implausible *statements* of some more or less widely held views. Darwin's theory of evolution boils down to the claim that some of your relatives are monkeys. The concept of God is that of an old man who dabbles in clay figures. The Christian view of eternal life is that when you leave this life you take up residence in another place which swings from cellar to ceiling from now on. These views are obviously farfetched and easily attacked. But they are caricatures of more profound views. They are *straw men*. They are, as the name suggests, cheap imitations of the "real thing". Hence, their refutation is irrelevant to the genuine article.

The *straw man* fallacy is often committed by attacking weak *arguments* for a view instead of easily accessible stronger ones. For example, it might be claimed that the *only* reason you should not steal from your neighbor is that years ago your parents taught you not to steal. Then, since your parents probably passed on what their parents passed on to them, etc., there just isn't much of a reason for you not to steal. This argument is a *straw man*. There are a number of more plausible arguments against stealing than "You were taught not to steel", such as stealing is morally wrong; thieves may be punished by fines, imprisonment, adverse public opinion. The refutation of the *straw man* is an *ignoratio elenchi*.

4.16   Pride

The fallacy of appealing to **pride** (*argumentum ad superbiam*) is committed when *pride* is used to persuade someone to accept some claim. People are proud of all kinds of things: countries, states, cities, families, houses, horses, dogs, cats, boats, and bats. You name it and someone is probably proud of it. If not yours, then *his*. According to the American theologian Reinhold Niebuhr, pride is *the* great sin of man. If it is, it is surely one that we pay for "in spades". Consider a few homely examples:

> You are proud of your country.
> You must buy savings bonds.

> You are proud of your home.
> It needs to be painted.

> You are proud of your girl friend.
> She deserves to be taken out to dinner.

On and on it goes. But the arguments are fallacious. It is possible to be proud of one's country without buying bonds. It is also possible to buy the bonds of a country of which one is ashamed. One could easily be proud of a home that does not need painting. Indeed, one might be proud of his home precisely because it did *not* need painting. And so far as your girl is concerned, well, what's the use? You couldn't convince her anyhow.

4.17   Good intentions

The fallacy of appealing to **good intentions** is committed when it is argued that because one's intentions or motives are good, one's claims are true, i.e.

> My intentions are good.
> Whatever I say is true.

Frequently, however, the question at issue is not one of truth or falsity but of right and wrong, fairness or unfairness, justice or injustice. That is,

> My intentions are good.
> Whatever I say (do) is right (fair, just).

seems to be a more typical form of the fallacy of *good intentions*.

Whether the question is one of truth or falsity or of morality, the fallacy is apparent. If *truth* followed good will, there would be fewer falsehoods uttered. Most students would find it difficult to fail any examinations. There would be no honest quacks or cranks. Those who meant well would *ipso facto* utter only true sentences. Similarly, if *justice* followed good will, there would be much less injustice than there is. The most heinous crimes are committed by men with only the highest motives. The Ku Klux Klan and the Nazi party are made up of men who are dedicated to keeping the races pure (preferably, I suppose, pure Nazi or pure Klan). As one Klansman put it, "We are dedicated to keeping the races just as God created them. Ain't that the way it *should* be"? Clearly, if truth or justice followed from *good intentions* we would have quite a different world.

4.18   Vacuous guarantees

The fallacy of appealing to **vacuous guarantees** is committed when the warrant offered for a claim is void of content, tautologous, or without substance. Typically, faulty guarantees are fairly substantial *on paper* but entirely vacuous *in practice*. For example, suppose it is claimed that Slashaway razor blades will give you more shaves per blade than ony other razor or your money back. This looks like a fairly bold claim. But it is completely *vacuous*, if, when the time comes to make it good, the honesty of the purchaser is questioned, or the vendor is unwilling to take the responsibility of refunding your money, or the producer cannot be easily contacted.

Again, the products that are supposed to last five years under "normal" use are *vacuously guaranteed* if in practice no one seems to use the gadget "normally". The wax that stays beautiful under "normal" conditions is *vacuously guaranteed* if in practice "normal" conditions never obtain. The gasoline guaranteed to keep your carburetor clean is *vacuously guaranteed* if the dirt always seems to arrive on the scene *before* you start using that kind of gasoline. Quite generally then, we might say that if the *costs* in time, energy, and money of getting a producer to stand behind his guarantee outweigh the cost of the *product*, the guarantee is *vacuous*.

4.19   Rationalization

The fallacy of **rationalization** is committed when a more or less *acceptable* reason for an action is substituted for the *real* reason. The substituted reason might be an observable physical cause or a fairly respectable motive. For example, suppose you have a blind date and you suspect that she is not attractive. You decide that the only way to prevent a wholly disastrous evening is to risk only *part* of it. You will pick her up two hours late. When you finally show up, she asks you why you are late. You supply a few false but plausible reasons, e.g., you had *two* flat tires; the guys at the fraternity house hid your clothes; you *thought* you told her 10 o'clock; you wanted to see how she would react. All these are irrelevant *rationalizations*.

People are frequently guilty of *rationalizing* their failures: Zip finished last in the race *because* he slipped coming off the starting blocks. Speedy placed fifth because he was upset about a history examination. Lightning beat only Speedy and Zip because he couldn't bear to hurt anyone else's feelings. Flash ran third because winning just wasn't important. Whizzer came in second because he was only a sophomore. The Tortoise won because there just wasn't any competition, etc.

4.20   Monday morning quarterbacking

In football, a game which is seldom played on Mondays, the quarterback is supposed to plan the offensive strategy. Sometimes, *after* a play has been poorly executed, it looks as if some other play should have been called. People who have a habit of explaining what should have been done and what would have happened *if* it had been done are called *Monday morning quarterbacks*. Now, since nobody knows what would have happened if what *did* happen did *not*, nobody knows what should have been done. We might have fairly good reasons for believing that such and such a play was the right one, but there is no way *now* to prove that it would have been right *then*. Those who insist that they know exactly what would have been the case *if* something else was the case or what would have happened *if* something else had happened commit the fallacy of **Monday morning quarterbacking.**

Suppose, for example, a historian claims that the Protestant Reformation could not have begun without Martin Luther. Another historian claims that the Reformation would have occurred with or without Luther. Both are committing the *Monday morning quarterbacking fallacy*, for there is no way to prove either claim. This is not to say that we cannot or should not try to gather evidence for either or both claims. The point is rather that much of the evidence must be *inconclusive* or *highly problematic* because much of it would have to be of the form "If *M* had not have happened then individual *A* would have done *P* instead of *Q*". "If *Q* occurred instead of *P* then *R* would have happened to individual *B* instead of *S*." etc. The fallacy consists in claiming to have *exact* and *certain* knowledge about a situation which does not admit of such knowledge.

4.21   Simple diversion

The fallacy of **simple diversion** (or the *red herring*) is committed when one attempts to secure his own position by directing attention away from its undesirable aspects. A realtor may commit the fallacy of *simple diversion* by changing the subject whenever the question of a down payment is raised. Instead of accounting for the puddles in the basement, he may call your attention to the beautiful landscape. He might meet questions about cracking plaster with remarks about lovely woodwork, etc.

This fallacy is often used against children. Instead of meeting their questions about why they cannot have this, that, or the other thing, we try to divert their attention. If they are pushing for a new bicycle, we ask them about school or about the forthcoming picnic. If the question is whether or not they can hold a pajama party, we try persuading them to have a picnic, etc. While it is a useful tactic to use against children, the fallacy of *simple diversion* should not fool too many adults.

Review problems for Secs. 4.15–4.21

I. Distinguish the following types of irrelevant appeals:

1. straw man
2. pride
3. good intentions
4. vacuous guarantees
5. rationalization
6. Monday morning quarterbacking
7. simple diversion

II.   Name and explain the type of irrelevant appeal involved in the following:

1.   CITIZEN: What's your view on the traffic bill?
     CANDIDATE: We must support our schools.
2.   SALESMAN: It *would* last three years under normal conditions, but how do I know you haven't been running it all over town.
3.   He can't be blamed. He was only trying to help.
4.   As far as I can see, the main argument for democracy is that Jefferson thought it was a good idea.
5.   If he would have kept his mouth shut, we wouldn't be here now and you wouldn't be changing that tire.
6.   It's *your* school. If that isn't enough incentive for you, I don't know what is
7.   I was going to study last night, but then Fred called and I figured my social life was important too, so I went out.
8.   WIFE: Did you carry out the garbage?
     HUSBAND: I just saw Charlie go by in a red Ford.
9.   If it doesn't give you better performance than the one you have, I'll eat my hat.
10. Sure Christianity is convincing, if you think a guy could walk on water.
11. It's up to you pal. If you want a garden neighbors will admire, you better believe me.
12. In the first place, he should have told his mother-in-law to go to hell. That would have solved everything.
13. But I can't brush my teeth after every meal. I don't have any place to put my toothbrush; besides, it doesn't make any difference anyhow.
14. FRANKIE: How about taking in a movie?
     JOHNNIE: I had two exams last Monday.
15. He really believes in what he's doing. It can't be all bad.

III.   Make up examples of each of the fallacies distinguished in Part I.

IV.   Comprehensive review problems for this entire chapter: Name and explain the type of irrelevant appeal involved in each.

1.   He ought to be satisfied with ten dollars; so he will be.
2.   Last night you were all for it, but today you're not so sure. That proves it's worthless.
3.   BOSS: Why haven't you finished washing the breakfast dishes?
     DISHWASHER: That ball game last night was terrific.
4.   I really don't care whether you hire us to trim your trees or not. If one of those huge dead branches falls throught the roof, it might kill someone. But that's your problem.
5.   SALESMAN: Get a new one. Aren't you ashamed of that rusty old jalopy?
6.   KING: Of course I should be king. After *all*, I am the King.

7. ABNER: What makes you so sure that's Mammy's pipe?
    DAISY MAE: No one has proved that it's not.

8. PROSECUTOR: The attorney for the defense is obviously interested in saving
    his client's neck. So you can't believe *him*.

9. If Moses hadn't have been such a tough cookie, the whole history of the
    world would have been different.

10. ABLE: But I have already shown you that we may derive a contradiction from
    those premisses *without* my claim.
    BAKER: Right! So your claim must be rejected.

11. My conscience is clear and I only want to help you out. So I can't go wrong.

12. Of course it's my turn. Or would you like a rap in the mouth?

13. If this ironing board breaks down in the next two years you can sue us. What
    more could you want?

14. ATTORNEY: Of course, if you want to believe the testimony of this alcoholic,
    this unstable reprobate, you may.

15. SCOUTMASTER: A scout learns useful things. For example, he learns how to
    start fires without matches.
    OBSERVER: If that is all scouting is, who needs it? You can buy matches
    anywhere.

16. That's Jesse James's grandson. Don't trust him.

17. LOSER: I wasn't really trying to win. Besides who cares anyhow?

18. If you're really my friend, you'll vote for me now.

19. CANDIDATE: I have promised to stick to the issues in this campaign. But don't
    forget that my opponent knows at least six members of the Communist party.

20. Psychoanalysis is worthless because it's based on the assumption that Sigmund
    Freud is the only guy in the world who ever understood sex.

21. STUDENT: When I'm lying in some muddy foxhole with trench foot, I'll
    remember how I got there. I ask you, sir, do I deserve that kind of suffering
    for failing a biology test?

22. CITIZEN: Will we have a tax increase this year?
    CANDIDATE: The first thing we must do is end the war.

23. I've never seen God, and that's proof enough for me that He doesn't exist.

chapter
five   CONFUSION

> *A man should make up his mind with emphasis as
> to what he rationally believes, and should
> never allow contrary irrational beliefs to pass
> unchallenged or obtain a hold over him,
> however brief.*   Bertrand Russell

When an argument or a view is presented in such a confused or ambiguous fashion that no one knows exactly what it means or that it might be used to prove two or more different things, we will say that a fallacy of **confusion** has been committed. A fallacy of *confusion* might be relevant or irrelevant to a question at issue. In the former case, it could not be considered an *irrelevant appeal*, but in the latter case, it could. Hence, whether or not a particular fallacy introduced in this section might be properly placed in the preceding one depends to some extent on the content of the fallacy itself. We will discuss fourteen specific ways to commit a fallacy of *confusion*, a fallacy which may properly be regarded as *informal*.

5.1   Equivocation

The fallacy of **equivocation** (*equivocatio* or *homonymia*) is committed when the double meaning of a term is played upon in a misleading or erroneous fashion. For example, suppose a philosopher claims that everything in the universe has some sort of experience because experience is nothing more than interaction, and everything in the universe interacts with something. Here the ambiguity of the term *interaction* has lead to the peculiar view that, say, tables and chairs have experiences. Tables and chairs may be said to *interact* in the sense that a chair cannot occupy the very same place at the same time a table is occupying it, i.e., tables and chairs are not entirely independent with respect to their spatial locations. People might interact in this sense *or* in the sense that they may exchange ideas by communicating with one another, Ordinarily, only this more or less conscious type of interaction is considered experience. The fallacy of *equivocation* has been committed by playing on these two different senses of *interaction*.

The terms *independent* and *dependent* are notoriously ambiguous. If someone informs you that Simon Butcher is independent, exactly what has he told you? Is he politically religiously, economically, or socially independent? Is he a free thinker or a free lover? Is he a lover of free thinking or does he just think about loving freely? The fallacy of *equivocation* would be committed if someone began with a premiss attributing independence in one sense to Butcher and concluded from that that Butcher possessed independence in an entirely different sense. Similarly, one might *equivocate* on the term *dependent* by fallaciously deriving, say, Butcher's economic dependence from his religious dependence.

5.2 Amphiboly

An *amphibolous* sentence is one that is ambiguous due to its peculiar structure. The fallacy of **amphiboly** (*fallacia amphibolia*) is committed when the amphibolous structure of a sentence is played upon in a misleading or erroneous fashion. Suppose, for example, you are in a restaurant and have just finished a delicious tossed salad. You call the manager to ask him what was in the dressing and who made it. The manager replies "The chef tossed the salad with greasy hair tonic". Hopefully, he meant to say that the chef who uses greasy hair tonic tossed the salad. But he might have been suggesting the ingredient for the dressing, namely greasy hair tonic. The fallacy of *amphiboly* is committed if one infers from the manager's reply that greasy hair tonic must have been used in the salad dressing.

Again, suppose someone advertises his automobile for sale with the following notice:

For Sale: 1964 Ford with automatic transmission,
radio, heater, power brakes, power
steering and windshield wipers in good condition.

When you inspect the car, you find that the windshield wipers are the *only* accessories that are in good condition. When you charge the vendor with misrepresentation, he replies, "You misread the ad. Read it again". The ad was *amphibolous*, and the vendor used it to commit the fallacy of *amphiboly*.

The attendant at a roulette wheel in an amusement park offered some naïve spectators "ten bets for a dollar". Because this sounded like a bargain, the spectators gave him the dollar. After the first bet was made and lost, they began to make a second. But the attendant insisted that they had misunderstood him. "Ten bets for a dollar", he explained "meant ten bets for a dollar *each*". This is another instance of the fallacy of *amphiboly*.

5.3   Accent

Sometimes a sentence takes on different meanings depending upon the ways in which it is *accented*. The fallacy of **accent** (*fallacia accentus*) is committed when an improperly accented false or misleading sentence is inferred from a sentence which is true if properly accented. For example, someone might infer from the principle

Men ought to be kind to strangers.

that *women* may treat strangers any old way and that both men and women may be mean to *friends*. Again, describing a football player who decided to sign a contract to play for another team, a coach said, "Oh, he's a good *football player*". While he was certainly that, the coach accented "football player" so we might infer fallaciously that he was *only* that, or that, all things considered, he was not worth signing anyhow.

The practice of emphasizing certain words in a quotation by using italics or by underscoring them when they were not so shown in the original text is supposed to eliminate the fallacy of *accent* from the written material. Thus if '*rose*' or '*smell*' is underlined or shown in italics in

A rose by any other name would smell as sweet.

one might infer fallaciously that Shakespeare was concerned primarily with roses or smells. However, this claim was supposed to illustrate his feeling about the essential attributes of things and of the inessential relation between these attributes and their names.

5.4 Humor

When someone uses humor to confuse his listeners or the question at issue, he commits the fallacy of confusion with **humor**. Suppose, for instance, that a student is trying to prove that men ought to do good rather than evil. He begins by assuming the existence of God. Maxwell Smart points out that the assumption is unwarranted and that it would be wiser to try to avoid it. The first student replies, "Only an evil person would say that, and, anyhow, then he would go straight to hell without passing 'Go' or collecting five hundred dollars". Presumably, Smart's objection was buried in laughter or as others have said, "lost in a laugh".

Instructors frequently resort to funny stories to avoid the admission of simplemindedness or error. Very often humorous cracks are substituted for sound criticism. Instead of telling a student *exactly* what is wrong with his history examination, an instructor might write "This is more hysterical than historical" in the margin. Or, "It's wonderful to see how well you've mastered your name. Don't you think it's time you tackled something else"? Or, "You're putting me on". To give us devils our due, it must be admitted sometimes it would be too painful or too wasteful to write out lengthy criticisms. But sometimes humor is introduced merely to avoid reflection on one's own inadequacies (e.g., a lack of precise grading criteria). In such cases the fallacy of confusion with *humor* is committed.

5.5 Contradictory assumptions

The fallacy of **contradictory assumptions** is committed when the premisses used in an argument are contradictory. Since one of two contradictory sentences must be false, the argument must contain a *false* premiss. Hence, it must be unsound. Moreover, *any* sentence whatever may be derived from a set of premisses that are inconsistent. Suppose, for example, someone is trying to prove that Canadians are more honest than New Zealanders. He begins with the assumption that people who live north of the Equator are honest. After some haggling, he admits that some Germans are not honest. His conclusion, that Canadians are more honest than New Zealanders, follows with certainty. But the victory is deceptive. The *denial* of his conclusion *also* follows with certainty. Hence, his argument is unsound. It is an instance of the fallacy of *contradictory assumptions*.

It seldom happens that obviously contradictory premises are asserted in an argument. Very often, however, people act in accordance with rules or principles which are contradictory but never made explicit enough to be discovered. The result of adhering to contradictory principles of action is, of course, that one is permitted (at least by *his own* principles) to do anything he pleases. Suppose, for example, a school administrator dismisses one teacher for being active in local politics and another for being inactive. When he explains his decision to the first teacher he suggests the principle that people who are active in politics should not be teachers. To the second teacher he announces the *contradictory* principle that people who are inactive in politics should not be teachers. As long as the two teachers or, perhaps, the school board, never examine the administrator's principles of behavior, his behavior is practically unrestricted. He can justify *any* sort of action by his *contradictory assumptions*. Hence, he has committed a fallacy of confusion with them.

5.6 Anger

When someone is confused or misled by anger, or attempts to confuse or mislead his listeners by angering them or by displaying signs of anger, he commits the fallacy of confusion with **anger**. Most people try to avoid angering and being angered by others. I suppose it has something to do with manners, socialization, cowardice, etc. Moreover, most people seem to become muddleheaded when they are emotionally disturbed by anger. Hence, in one way or another *anger* may be used to create confusion. For example, suppose you present an argument to someone who finds the conclusion unacceptable. He might begin his attack by insulting you; perhaps he might call you 'a stupid ass'. If you are not expecting it, you might be thrown completely off the track. You might forget your line of argumentation and reply to his *insult*. In certain contexts, say, in a public debate, he may gain enough time to think of a legitimate objection. At least he might confuse the issue enough to pass to another and avoid the admission of defeat. However, if you have your wits about you, you may easily destroy his trick by pointing out the fact that he has committed a fallacy of confusion with *anger*.

In a similar situation, someone might feign anger himself. He might make it appear as if you were attacking him, i.e., make it appear as if your argument were an instance of *abusing the man*. This might give him more time or perhaps force you to completely withdraw your argument. Although he might gain some advantage in either case, he would still be committing the fallacy of confusion with *anger*.

5.7   Lack of understanding

One way to escape the conclusion of a powerful argument or to *a priori* reject the legitimacy of some view is to claim complete *lack of understanding*. This seems to be a favorite move of philosophers when they are considering doctrines they do not share. Scientifically oriented positivists or empiricists very often find the arguments and views of theologians and existentialists completely *incomprehensible*. Now, a claim might be beyond the comprehension of most people because it is profound or because it is meaningless or nonsensical. Needless to say, those who plead total lack of understanding usually imply in tone or manner that the claim in question is *not* profound. Those who claim complete lack of understanding in order to avoid coming to grips with an issue or to confuse issues by repeatedly requiring alternative statements of them commit the fallacy of confusion with **lack of understanding**.

Consider, for example, the claim that there is at least one *necessary* being, namely God. Those who defend this notion generally define the term 'necessary being' as a being which is self-explanatory, or a being which contains within itself the reason for its own existence, or a being which cannot *not* exist, or a being whose essence it is to exist, etc. Such a being is contrasted with beings that are *not* self-explanatory, e g., people require parents. Now, some philosophers attack this view on the ground that the idea of a necessary being is meaningless. The notion must be meaningless, they say, because only sentences (or perhaps propositions) can be necessary. Hence, there is no need to consider any argument which leads to the conclusion that a necessary being exists. This is a fallacy of confusion with *lack of understanding* unless some good reason is offered to apply the term 'necessary' only to sentences (or propositions) or to define it in such a way that it cannot be used in any other context. While it might be true that the various alternative *definitions* of the term 'necessary being' are incomprehensible, their meaninglessness does *not follow* from the fact that some people prefer to apply the term 'necessary' only to sentences. To suppose otherwise without a proof is to commit the fallacy of *lack of understanding*.

Since we cannot open a person's skull, as it were, to find out whether or not he is genuinely confused, it may often be difficult to know when this fallacy is committed. Furthermore, there is no generally accepted criterion of meaningfulness which might be applied to reach an objective, independent, or unbiased judgment about the meaningfulness of any sentence. Philosophers frequently appeal to stock phrases. But such usage has not yet produced an uncontroversial basic vocabulary, and there seems to be no reason to suspect any change in this situation in the future. It seems, therefore, that the fallacy of confusion with *lack of understanding* will remain a fairly viable and practically undetectable trick for some time to come.

Review problems for Secs. 5.1–5.7

I. Distinguish the following fallacies of confusion:

1. equivocation
2. amphiboly
3. accent
4. humor
5. contradictory assumptions
6. anger
7. lack of understanding

II. Name and explain the *type* of confusion involved in the following:

1. I know he's guilty. If he confesses that proves it. If he doesn't confess he's hiding his guilt.
2. I have never used the word that way. Consequently you're not making sense.
3. STUDENT: Of course I know the answer, but since you insist on insulting me, I'm not talking.
4. ALCOHOLIC: Will my wife leave me?
   PSYCHIATRIST: Men who drink more often than not lose their wives.

5. PRIEST: It is written, "Thou shalt not kill".
    ACCOMPLICE: *I* didn't disobey the commandment. I paid someone else to do the killing.
6. BLONDIE: Was he mad because you spilled your coffee on him?
    DAGWOOD: Yes, he was.
    BLONDIE: Then you should have had him locked up like any other madman.
7. EXAMINER: You have one more minute to answer the question.
    STUDENT: I resent that remark. You're trying to make me panic.
8. AMATEUR: Isn't this drink something else?
    PROFESSIONAL: I'll say, it's *something* else.
9. DEAN: Young man, you are the first person who has ever dumped a pail of water on me. I want an explanation.
    STUDENT: At least now no one can say you're a dirty old man.
10. WIFE: I say we need a new refrigerator.
    HUSBAND: And I say you sound just like your dumb, freeloading mother.
11. When I use the word "theology", I mean discourse about God. If you don't mean that then as fas as I'm concerned you're not making any sense, and we have nothing to talk about.
12. PROPHET: The end of the world is coming next week.
    CLIENT: That's what you said last week.
    PROPHET: So, next week we'll see if I was right. Right?
13. DEZI: All men are created equal.
    LUCY: Then why isn't my opinion worth anything in this house?
    DEZI: Because you're not a *man*, obviously.
14. MUTT: I would like to see the old woman with the silver legs.
    JEFF: What makes you think anyone here has silver legs.
    MUTT: Because your ad said that a coffee table belonging to an old woman with silver legs was for sale.
15. SON: When I took her out you got mad, and when I didn't take her out you still got mad. What do you expect me to do?
    FATHER: Just don't do things that make me angry.
16. MAN: Do you know the answer or not?
    POLITICIAN: Yes, but did anyone ever tell you you're beautiful when you're angry.
17. The end of life is happiness. Since death is the end of life, death is happiness.

III. Make up examples of each of the fallacies distinguished in Part I.

5.8 Trivial objections

The fallacy of confusion with **trivial objections** is committed when someone supposes or asserts that *any* objection to a view or argument is sufficient to overthrow it. There are surely few if any claims that are not open to *some* kind of objection. But some objections are less significant than others and it is more reasonable to accept *tentatively slightly* objectionable claims, hypotheses, or theories than to reject them. For example, it would have been a mistake to reject Einstein's theory of relativity on the ground that it was incomprehensible to the average layman. Again, it would have been a mistake to reject Freudian psychology on the ground that it offended certain people's notions about sex, religion, and parenthood. In cases like these, one must weigh the significance of the objection against the total import of the view attacked. Admittedly, this may put quite a strain on one's philosophic or scientific conscience, but the alternative of abandoning otherwise respectable views in the face of *trivial objections* is surely unacceptable.

It should be mentioned, perhaps, that the main differences between this fallacy and that of the *straw man* is that here a weaker view is *not* substituted for the view allegedly attacked. Here the view under attack is presented properly but contains certain more or less *trivial* flaws. It is then insisted that these infelicities are sufficient to disprove the view in question. The fallacy, quite simply put, is that of supposing that a trivial objection is not trivial.

5.9   Emotional language

The fallacy of confusion with **emotional language** is committed when, without increasing the supporting evidence for a view, the view is made more *persuasive* by the use of *emotional* language. For example, suppose a girl is trying to convince her father that she is ready to marry and leave home. She could approach him with this: "Father, I am ready to marry and leave home." On the other hand, she could spice it up a little like this: "Oh Daddy, I'm so much in love with Lorenzo. I love his smile, the way he walks, and the way he smells. I want him to be the father of my children. I want to grow old with him, to be by him forever". The second approach does not contain any more *evidence* for her view than the first, but the second (some would say) is more *persuasive*.

Again, consider the difference in force of the following descriptions:

> Herman's arm was cut above his left elbow.
> Herman's arm was slashed open to the bone.

These two descriptions of Herman's injury might both be accurate, but the second sounds more serious. If one were prosecuting the man who put the knife to Herman, one might prefer the second description. If one were defending him, the first would be more attractive. Insofar as the second account would tend to confuse the issue by provoking an emotional response, the fallacy of confusion with *emotional language* would be committed.

5.10   Pseudoarguments

Some people never seem to be at a loss for words. Given any problem, faced with any question, they seem to have a gift of always being able to respond at length! Some of these people are quick-witted and articulate enough to carry on a high level conversation on many different topics at a rapid, but thoroughly responsible pace. However, there are others who lack this gift but have developed the art of *appearing* to have it. These people frequently confuse us by talking around, beside, beyond, beneath, and above a point and then announcing some presumably relevant conclusion as if it followed from all that preceded it. Their strategy is extremely effective primarily, I am convinced, because most of us *suppose* that when someone is talking, he is making sense. We *expect* him to make sense, at least to himself. Hence, if it seems that he is in fact talking gibberish, our first reaction is to suspect *we* are somehow limited or slow. We immediately tend to put the burden of comprehension on ourselves. (Recall for a moment your feeling when your instructor says he does not understand your question.) Rarely are most of us so sure of ourselves that our first impression is to suspect the *other fellow* of being muddleheaded.

Again then, we have a case in which a particular human frailty may be used to deceive people. Perhaps by assigning a name to this type of deception, its appearance will be curtailed. Hence, let us say that when someone claims to derive a conclusion from gibberish or scrambled linguistic expressions, he is committing a fallacy of confusion with **pseudoarguments**. For example, consider the following piece of philosophic gibberish:

> Beyond the solid sea of Being there lies
> the bottomless pit of Nothingness into
> which the trembling souls of men are cast.

> Nothingness and Being wage an eternal holy
> war against each other. For every soul
> snatched up by Nothingness, one must be
> created by Being. Therefore, every man
> must live in fear of the unknown.

The premisses of this argument consist of pure and poor poetic poppycock, and the presumably (but by no means obviously) relevant conclusion is, therefore, standing on its own meager merits. This is typical of the fallacy of *pseudoarguments*.

5.11   Etymology

The fallacy of confusion with **etymology** is committed when it is argued that a term must be used in such and such a way or mean this or that because once upon a time it (or a word from which it was derived) was used in such and such a way or meant this or that. For example, someone might argue that it is a mistake to give historians, philosophers, or mathematicians the title of 'doctor' because the Romans reserved it for physicians. Whether or not the claim is historically accurate, a fallacy of confusion with *etymology* would be committed. When in the U.S.A. one need not do as the Romans did. Similarly, it would be a mistake to assert that atoms must be simple and indivisible because the word 'atom' comes from the Greek word *ātomos*, meaning indivisible. Finally, the fallacy of confusion with *etymology* would be committed if one argued that psychology could not or should not be the study of human *behavior* because 'psycho' is derived from the Greek *psychē* meaning breath, spirit, or mind. It is false as a matter of fact that psychology is not largely (if not totally) the study of human behavior. Perhaps it would be wrong for it to be what it is if it were supposed to be what the Greeks thought it should be, but there is no reason to suppose that psychology should be what the Greeks thought it should be.

5.12   Exceptions to the rule

There is a misleading aphorism which runs, "The exception proves the rule". This seems to mean that we may establish the *applicability* of a rule by finding an exception to it, or that we may demonstrate the *truth* of a generalization by finding a contradictory case or counterinstance of it. Such claims are not only confusing; they are patently false.

If a counterinstance of a generalization is found, the generalization is falsified, e.g., we falsify 'all men are green' by finding at least one man who is not green. Rules cannot be true or false, but they can be applicable or inapplicable. The rule 'this door must be closed at all times' does not have a truth-value any more than the command 'close the door' and the question 'Is the door closed?' have truth-values. However, rules, like commands and questions, do have *scopes* of application. For example, 'this door must be closed at all times' is the sort of rule one might write on a door, but not the sort of rule one would write on a rosebush. Similarly, 'close the door' is a senseless command unless there is a door nearby and it is open.

Now, if someone claims that either generalizations or rules are established by the discovery of exceptions, we will say he has committed a fallacy of confusion called **exceptions to a rule**. For example, consider the rule of etiquette which says that a gentleman should stand up when a lady enters the room. If some generally recognized authority on etiquette rejected this rule, that would *not* demonstrate its acceptability. On the contrary, it would tend to undermine it or show its inapplicability. Hence, if someone claimed that this exception proved the rule, he would be committing the fallacy of *exceptions to a rule*.

One might say that by introducing exceptions to a rule, the proper scope of application of the rule is determined, i.e., exceptions delineate the scope of rules. For example, no one would expect a bedridden or crippled gentleman to attempt to stand up in the presence of a lady. The rule does not apply to such exceptional cases. But such cases *are* used to delineate the scope of the rule in a fairly illustrative way.

5.13   *Answering questions with questions*

The fallacy of *answering questions with questions* is similar to but distinct from that of shifting the burden of proof by *appealing to ignorance*. In the latter case, a "Why?" was met by a "Why not?" Here the "Why?" might be met with another "Why?" or "Who?" or "What?" That is, when a legitimate (not, for example, a *complex* or leading) question is answered with another question, the fallacy of confusion by **answering**

questions with questions is committed. Consider the following conversation between two Zen Buddhists:

> David: How is the sound of one hand clapping?
>
> Chet: How does a square look without corners?
>
> David: How soft is it?
>
> Chet: How square is it?
>
> David: Have you heard it?
>
> Chet: Have you seen it?
>
> David: Good night Chet.
>
> Chet: Good night David.

It is doubtful that either Chet or David has anything to say, and it is
certain that both are simply failing to make any assertions at all. Both are
merely questioning questions and, since questions cannot be true or false,
such persistent questioning cannot be informative. As a method of search-
ing for truth or of deriving true sentences from other true sentences, the
method is completely worthless. The question of truth or falsity never
even enters the picture.

Although it cannot be denied that persistent questioning often leads
to new knowledge, it must be remembered that questions are means to
this important end and *not* the end itself. Endless rhetorical questioning
is no substitute for knowledge and it is a fallacy of confusion to *answer
questions with questions* as if that were a mark of wisdom or mysterious
profundity.

5.14   Alleged ambiguity

We have seen that a sentence might be ambiguous because it contains
ambiguous terms or perhaps a peculiar structure. But no explicit criterion
of ambiguity has been suggested. Indeed, there does not appear to be one.
That is to say, there seems to be no criterion which one could apply to
ordinary English sentences to determine once and for all whether or not
they are ambiguous. Sentences which are unambiguous in one context
may be ambiguous in another. Sentences which seem perfectly straightforward to one person might be confusingly ambiguous to another. This
sort of thing happens every day and it lays the foundation for a rather

shrewd kind of deception. If a view has been fairly demolished, one might insist that it is after all ambiguous, and that while the objections *do* apply to the view interpreted in *one* way, they are completely irrelevant to the view interpreted in *another* way. If the ambiguity cited has been inrtoduced or invented *ad hoc* in order to prevent the rejection of the view, it is bound to lead to confusion. Hence, let us say that if, in order to preserve one's position, one *pretends* that it might be interpreted in more than one way and that the way it *should* be interpreted is unobjectionable, a fallacy of confusion with **alleged ambiguity** is committed.

Suppose, for example, Roger Ramjet claims that everything is water. This sounds peculiar to Mrs. Ramjet. She asks, "What about sticks and stones and bones, dear? Surely, you do not want to say that they are water!" Roger thinks for a moment and replies that when it is said that everything is water one may interpret the claim in a number of ways: Everything *might* be (essentially) water; everything might *seem* to be water to someone; everything *is* water to someone; everthing *should* be water; etc. Then he points out that his claim must be interpreted in the sense that everything *seems* to be water to someone, namely, Roger Ramjet. He has committed the fallacy of *alleged ambiguity*. It is doubtful that anyone but Roger would suggest 'everything seems to be water to Roger Ramjet' as a legitimate interpretation of the sentence 'everything is water'. Surely the former does not follow from the latter, i.e., the latter *could* be true and the former false. Perhaps some historians of philosophy would be willing to admit 'everything seems to be water to Thales' as a legitimate interpretation, but even that seems to be stretching things too far. 'Everything is water' is perfectly straightforward and false. Hence, if someone pretends it is ambiguous and true, the fallacy of confusion with *alleged ambiguity* is committed.

Review problems for Secs. 5.8–5.14

I. Distinguish the following fallacies of confusion:

1. trivial objections
2. emotional language
3. psuedoarguments
4. etymology
5. exceptions to a rule
6. answering questions with questions
7. alleged ambiguity

II.　Name and explain the type of confusion involved in the following:

1.　The word 'theology' comes from the Greek words meaning discourse about God. Hence, an atheistic theology is a plain contradiction.

2.　NANCY: Would you say that painting is beautiful?
SLUGGO: Would you say that painting is not beautiful?

3.　The universal principles of suction and pressure are polar principles. When the degree of suction is exactly 3.147 times that of the degree of pressure and the barometer is rising, it follows that you must have an argument with a policeman.

4.　I know it reduced pain in 99 cases out of 100. But one patient in every hundred will get an upset stomach. That means the product is just not acceptable.

5.　Aha! He *quit* smoking. That proves my point. Everyone smokes.

6.　STUDENT: So I looked on his paper.
TEACHER: You didn't just "look on his paper". You schemed and plotted and planned to deceive me. You let down your fellow students, your parents, your priest. You're a foul creature, a foolish, phoney, foul creature.

7.　STANLEY: Are you happy with the state of the world?
OLIVER: Are *you* happy with the state of the world?

8.　No, "ham" is sometimes used to refer to the leg of a chicken, and if you use *that* interpretation, what I said is true.

9.　In the absence of coercion from the throne, it is possible for the rich landlords to resist taxation. Those who suffer most are the peasants. Clearly, therefore, communism is superior to democracy.

10.　"Philosophy" comes from the Greek words meaning lover of wisdom. So that's what philosophers are, wisdom-lovers.

11.　MATHEMATICIAN: I can understand your enthusiam after discovering a proof that others have been seeking for a hundred years, but unfortunately most people will not be able to follow it. So I can't accept it.

12.　There's one slacker in every crew and that just goes to show that people really do believe in giving a full day's work for a full day's pay.

13.　Lots of people call their cousins "sister". If you look at it that way, he's right.

14.　Yes, I need a new hat. I need it to be able to hold my head up high, to be able to walk in the sunlight instead of in perpetual gloom. I need it to feel young again, to be part of the eternal reawakening of the universe.

15.　Sometimes "probable" means certain, and if you interpret the word that way, my claim is true.

16.　It's a great theory except for the fact that a Frenchman made it up.

III.　Make up examples of each of the fallacies distinguished in Part I.

IV.　Comprehensive review questions for this entire chapter: Name and explain the types of fallacy of confusion involved in the following.

1.　ABLE: Harry mopped the floor with his wife.
BAKER: Didn't it hurt her?

2. I know *you* never did that. That proves my point. Everyone does it.
3. "Democracy" sometimes means government by a single wealthy man.
4. "God exists" does not meet my criterion of meaningfulness. So it is nonsense.
5. Sweetheart, Love of my life, don't you want to put out the garbage?
6. IKE: Why do you want to go?
   MIKE: Why do you want to stay?
7. FRED: All men are mortal.
   ETHEL: Terrific! Then I'll live forever.
8. The book is fine, but I object to it because of its Preface.
9. I really don't remember what he said. He made me laugh and I forgot my objection.
10. Football used to be the name of only one game, a game that didn't include forward passes. So what we call "football" is not football at all.
11. I asked him to run for that office, and he turned around and ran towards my office. I guess he misunderstood my request.
12. How do I know what he said? After he insulted me I just turned red and forgot my reply.
13. TOM: With her tail between her legs the woman chased the dog down the street.
    DICK: Women don't have tails, so that can't be true.
14. It's a military necessity because our vital fluids are being sapped. The liquid ground of our being in Mother Nature's womb must be defended at all costs. Hence, we must attack.
15. I can't argue with that guy. Every time I corner him, he redefines words so he comes out ahead.

chapter

six FAULTY CLASSIFICATION

A man who has committed a mistake and doesn't correct it is committing another mistake. Confucius

The fallacies introduced in this chapter may be roughly distinguished by their particular relevance to the formation of classes, groups, sets, or collections of more or less similar things. They are blunders most frequently committed in such classificatory contexts. Aristotle believed that philosophy was the art of discovering similarities where there are to all appearances only differences, and of finding differences where there are apparently only similarities. This seems to be a fair description of most thinking, i.e., we are always ascribing certain predicates to certain subjects or withholding them. We are always putting things together, as it were, or taking them apart. Therefore, it is likely that we succumb to these fallacies more often than any others. The fallacies are *informal*.

6.1 Continuum

The fallacy of the **continuum** is committed when it is argued that because there is a continuous distribution of differences between two extremes, there is no "real" difference. For example, it might be argued that because there is a continuous distribution of differences between good and evil, nothing is "really" good or evil. Since there is no abrupt and obvious dichotomy between good and evil, there is supposed to be no "real" dichotomy at all.

Similarly, it has been argued that there is no "real" difference between what we ordinarily call 'consciousness' and 'unconsciousness' because EEG (electroencephalogram) patterns display more or less continuous changes. On this view, only dead people are completely unconscious. Whether or not it would be more profitable in the long run to adopt this rather extraordinary usage of the terms 'conscious' and 'unconscious', it is surely a fallacy to suppose that there are no important or "real" differences between the ordinary referents of these terms. The whole history of anesthesia sufficiently demonstrates this fact. Quite generally then, whenever it is argued that extremes are unimportant or "unreal" because there is a whole *continuum* of differences between them, the fallacy of the *continuum* is committed.

6.2   Golden mean

Given two extreme and conflicting views, it is often wise to select a position midway between them. For example, it might be wiser to invest half of one's savings than to invest all or none of them, or it might be more prudent to drink three martinis than six or none. However, the fallacy of the **golden mean** is committed when it is argued that the mean or middle view between two extremes must be true or right simply because it *is* the mean or middle view. For example, if a man dislikes martinis, he should drink something else or, perhaps, not drink at all. If he argues that given a choice of six, three, or no martinis, he should prefer the mean because it *is* the mean, he commits the fallacy of the *golden mean*. Similarly, the most promising place to be when you run out of gas is not midway between two cities, and the middle of the road is not the best place to drive. There is, in short, nothing *golden* about some means.

6.3   False dilemma

When someone has to choose one of two or more alternatives (frequently equally unpleasant ones) we say he is faced with a **dilemma.** The fallacy of **false dilemma** is committed when it is erroneously assumed or argued that one of two or more views must be true. For example, some people claimed that the United States had only two honorable alternatives in Viet Nam. It could have remained completely aloof from the battle or it could have become thoroughly involved in it. The fallacy of *false dilemma* is committed by failing to recognize a position somewhere between these two alternatives, e.g., perhaps the commitment of a limited number of supplies. Again, suppose someone is trying to get his education financed. He might commit the fallacy of *false dilemma* by claiming that he must go either to college or to the gutter. Not only are there a few steps between these two alternatives, it is also true that they are not mutually exclusive, i.e., some college people end up in the gutter and some gutter people end up in college.

6.4 Composition

The fallacy of **composition** is committed when it is argued that a property which is affirmed or denied of every part of some whole must be affirmed or denied of the whole. For example, one might argue that people are very small because people are made of cells, and cells are very small. In this case, the property of being small is erroneously attributed to a whole organism *because* it is attributed to its constituent parts. Similarly, one might argue that pipelines must be short because they are made of short segments, i.e., the property of being short is erroneously attributed to the whole line because it is attributed to each part of the line. Again, it might be argued that songs do not have melodies because they are made of individual notes which do not have melodies, i.e., the property of being melodious is withheld from whole songs because it is withheld from individual notes.

6.5 Division

The fallacy of **division** is committed when one argues that a property which is affirmed or denied of a *whole* must be affirmed or denied of each of its parts. For example, a philosopher might claim that subatomic particles must be intelligent because people are intelligent. (To which one is tempted to reply that some of them must be pregnant because some women are pregnant.) Similarly, one might infer that every page of a book is heavy because the book is heavy, that every member of a team is good because the team is good, etc.

6.6   Oversimplification

Among our fallacies of faulty classification there is one which is so familiar that it is adequately described as soon as it is named, that is, **oversimplification**. Few of us have not fallen prey to this fallacy. We find ourselves blaming a single man, usually Hitler, for the Second World War; or praising a single ballplayer for a team's victory; or regretting a single mistake as the one that *really* "broke the camel's back", etc. We attribute, say, Edison's success to his perseverance, as if his imagination and intellect were somehow incidental. We like to see people with less ability and opportunity turn out to be champions or presidents "by the sweat of their brows". In this respect most of us identify with the tortoise rather than the hare. But we are guilty of gross *oversimplification* if we assume that a single admirable characteristic is the cause of success. A multitude of actions, decisions, repercussions, reactions are built into every man's history, and his success or failure must be considered a complex function of all of them, not of just one of them.

6.7   Vague terms

The fallacy of **vague terms** is committed when one uses obscure, imprecise, or vague terms to substantiate unwarranted claims. For example, consider the case of an old woman who claimed that Robert Maynard Hutchins, the former Chancellor of the University of Chicago, should be fired for being "liberal". The term 'liberal', like its opposite 'conservative', may be applied in a number of different contexts (political, educational, religious, etc.), and *even when the context is clear*, the term lacks any specific, universally accepted content. (In this respect *vague* terms differ from *ambiguous* ones, because the *sense* in which the latter are to be understood *may* be clarified by the context.) That is to say, the term 'liberal' is so *vague* that no one could tell what Hutchins was being accused of. This, of course, makes *refutation* virtually impossible. Hence, unless some specific meaning is given to such a term, almost any sort of classifications and all sorts of confusion are apt to arise. Similarly, such terms as 'radical', 'free', 'reasonable', 'desirable', 'reliable', should be carefully defined before they are used. 'Francis is free', for instance, is uninformative unless a particular context is given and a particular sort of freedom is specified, e.g., free to go swimming, to have a drink, or to dance until dawn. He who fails to define such terms opens himself to the charge of committing the fallacy of *vague terms*.

6.8   Illicit contrast

The fallacy of **illicit contrast** is committed when it is argued that if an object has (lacks) a certain property, any contrary or contrasting object must lack (have) that property, For example, it might be argued that because only a *courageous* person would risk his life to save a friend, only a *coward* would *not* risk his life to save a friend. Again, someone might argue that if *women* are patient, *men* must be *im*patient. If young people are vigorous, old people must be lethargic, etc. If we permitted this sort of argumentation, we should have to say that people who are awake can do no good because people who are asleep can surely do no evil. That, of course, is ridiculous.

Review problems for Secs. 6.1–6.8

I.   Distinguish the following fallacies of faulty classification:

1. continuum
2. golden mean
3. false dilemma
4. composition
5. division
6. oversimplification
7. vague terms
8. illicit contrast

II.   Name and explain the type of faulty classification involved in the following:

1. The car *can't* go over 120 miles per hour and I *won't* go under 40. So I guess 80 miles per hour is exactly right.
2. I'll tell you why he won't go out with you. You're unreasonable. That's right, unreasonable!

3. There's no way out. If I can't buy a Cadillac, I'll just have to walk.
4. Tennis is a crazy game. The winner jumps over the net, but the loser doesn't crawl underneath it.
5. That team must be loaded with stars. They haven't lost a game yet.
6. I don't see how that team can lose. It's loaded with stars.
7. There can't be any real difference between science and art because the methods of each gradually shade into the other.
8. The trouble with Harry is that he's odd. That's why Elsa is afraid of him.
9. I knew you would want black coffee, Aunt Hazel, because Uncle John wants cream and sugar.
10. What's so special about sewing on a guy's arm? All you have to do is match up the loose ends and stitch 'em together.
11. The most beautiful note in the world is middle C because it's not too high and it's not too low. It's just right in the middle, where it ought to be.
12. WIFE: Either you don't love me or you're just a tightwad. Why else wouldn't you take me to the theater?
13. In the spring a young man's fancy turns to thoughts of love. That's why they're so hateful in the fall.
14. That sorority must be beautiful, because every girl in it is beautiful.
15. ETHEL: All the elephants in the zoo would cover a whole tennis court.
    FRED: I didn't know they made elephants that big.
16. All the problems of the world could be solved if men had only a little good will.
17. People's motives come in all shades. So there aren't any purely good or purely evil motives.

III. Make up examples of each of the fallacies distinguished in Part I.

chapter

seven   POLITICAL
FALLACIES

> *The ultimate measure of a man is not where he*
> *stands in moments of comfort and convenience,*
> *but where he stands at times of challenge and*
> *controversy.*   Martin Luther King, Jr.

We may say that an event or situation has **political significance** if it is directly related to the policies, laws, or principles governing one or more persons. Broadly speaking then, any sort of deception or mistake made in an argument that has political significance is a **political fallacy.** All the political fallacies introduced in this chapter are *informal*. Most of them were described by the great British philosopher Jeremy Bentham in his *Handbook of Political Fallacies* (1824). They are certainly not the *only* fallacies that may be committed in political contexts. Indeed, *all* the fallacies considered so far *might* occur in political contexts. Perhaps the most that should be claimed for the ones presented here is that they seemed particularly conspicuous to Bentham. As many of the examples will show, they may be committed on grand scales affecting whole nations or on somewhat lesser scales affecting only a handful of people, such as a small family or even single individuals.

7.1   The end justifies the means

The view that *every* means may be justified to reach a particular end or goal is traditionally known as the fallacy that **the end justifies the means.**

Suppose, for example, someone decides that world peace is his goal. Surely this is as altruistic an ambition as one could imagine, i.e., it is an exceptionally good *end*. The fallacy that *the end justifies the means* would be committed if he resigned himself to taking *every* available *means* to achieve this end. For in sanctioning *all* measures, he would be sanctioning even heinous ones, e.g., the obliteration of most or all of the human race. Similarly, while the goal of becoming a doctor is honorable, it could not be used to justify criminal behavior. Again, the goal of eliminating human disease is respectable, but it could not be used to justify the elimination of people as if they were guinea pigs. Finally, it should be noted that the fallacy that *the end justifies the means* is committed by those who argue or assume that a college degree is a goal that is good enough to warrant *any* sacrifice. Although it is doubtless fitting and proper for *some* people to go through college, it is equally true that it is *hardly ever* (*probably never*) worth driving yourself or anyone else crazy. After all, a college degree is *not* a ticket to paradise.

7.2　No precedent

Given practically any proposed innovation, it seems that there are always a few who take the view that if it has not been instituted by now, it is not worth instituting or, indeed, its institution would be downright harmful. Now, when a new law, policy, or action of any sort is introduced and someone argues that simply because there is *no precedent* for it, it is unacceptable, the fallacy of **no precedent** is committed. Thus, for example, those who first advocated laws for the prevention of cruelty to dumb animals and children were met by the *no precedent* fallacy. Such laws, it was supposed, had never been (thought) necessary before, so they were eternally unnecessary. Moreover, they required fundamental changes in people's behavior and attitudes toward such creatures, changes that could only be regarded as totally *unprecedented* and, therefore, unacceptable. Again, there are those who commit the *no precedent* fallacy by arguing that teachers should not engage in collective bargaining because there is little or *no precedent* for such involvement. On the contrary, however, even in those communities or institutions in which it is true that collective bargaining is unprecedented, there is frequently a *need* for such involvement, and where the need is present, the presence or absence of precedents must be considered irrelevant.

7.3 Novelty

The fallacy of **novelty** is committed by those who argue that a view, law, or policy which is novel, is *ipso facto* good. Those who commit the fallacy of *novelty* take an exactly opposite position toward unprecedented views as those who commit the *no precedent* fallacy. The latter moved fallaciously from 'it is new' to 'it is bad', and the former move equally fallaciously from 'it is new' to 'it is good'. Since *novelty* itself is neither inherently good nor inherently evil, such reasoning must be fallacious. Clearly, *not* every new idea is a good idea any more than every new product is a good product or every newborn infant is bound to turn out to be a saint.

7.4 Stagnation

The fallacy of **stagnation** is committed by those who argue that a view, law, or policy which is old is *ipso facto* bad, i.e., those who commit the fallacy of *stagnation* take a position toward traditionally accepted views which is exactly the opposite of that taken by those who commit the fallacy of appealing to *tradition*. The latter moved fallaciously from 'it is old' to 'it is good', and the former move equally fallaciously from 'it is old' to 'it is bad'. Certainly, there are plenty of good old ideas, e.g., that governors should rule by consent of the governed, that the planets move in roughly elliptical orbits, that a spoonful of sugar helps the medicine go down.

7.5 Imposter terms

The fallacy of **imposter terms** is committed when, in order to make an unpopular or plainly unacceptable view appear popular or acceptable, one simply gives the view a popular or acceptable name. For example, totalitarian governments, whether Communistic, fascistic, or whatever, might be called 'People's Governments' or 'Liberation Fronts', etc. While such traditional names as, say, 'fascist' would be treated with suspicion and distrust, such sweet sounding epithets as, say, 'The People's Republic' seem fairly innocuous. Again, it has been said, "In love and diplomacy you should never say 'no'. If you mean 'no', say 'yes' or 'maybe'. Then behave negatively when no one is looking or when whoever is looking is powerless or disinterested". Here 'yes' and 'maybe' are functioning as *imposter terms*. Finally, if someone happens to be an atheist in an area where atheism is unpopular, he might commit the fallacy of imposter terms by calling himself a 'Protestant', or a 'Catholic', or a 'Jew'. Quite generally then, whenever an unattractive view is made to appear attractive by using deceptive descriptions or names the fallacy of *imposter terms* is committed.

7.6   Special pleading

The fallacy of **special pleading** is committed when instead of presenting all the evidence or information one has about some view, one presents only a *special part* of it. More precisely, a *special pleader* presents only the information that is *favorable* to his own position. Hence, for example, a used-car salesman might describe the beautiful upholstery of an automobile, but fail to mention the car's defective transmission, i.e., he makes the case for his sales price as strong as possible by neglecting to mention any unfavorable information.

One who applies so-called universally applicable principles to everyone but himself is also a *special pleader*. For example, the history of higher education in America is full of cases in which men who had spent years advocating limited powers for college presidents began their *own* presidential careers by demanding complete autonomy for themselves. Similarly, at lower levels of administration we find that men who argue that deans should be subject to faculty review boards frequently resist the idea after they become deans.

7.7   Repeated assertion

The fallacy of **repeated assertion** is committed when it is argued or assumed that if a claim is repeated often enough, it becomes true. Totalitarian rulers in the twentieth century have been notorious practitioners of this deception. The Nazi party leaders of Hitler's Germany hammered away at the lies that the Jews had ruined the country and that they had to be eliminated. The more the lies were preached, the more the middle-of-the-roaders began to believe them.

The tactic has also been used in Communist countries against the United States, for example. Consider the all-out hate campaign initiated by the Chinese Communists. Many Chinese probably believe that the Americans are imperialists and ought to be feared, distrusted, and hated, because they have heard it so often and because they have never heard it denied. These people have fallen prey to the fallacy of *repeated assertion*.

We frequently encounter and/or commit this fallacy on a much smaller scale. If someone ignores or challenges our views, very often our first reaction is simply to *reassert* them. Perhaps, we suppose, we did not express ourselves very well, or the listener did not hear exactly what was said. When we continue to reassert our position after it is clear that neither of these possibilities has occurred, we are committing the fallacy of *repeated assertion*.

7.8 Quietism

The fallacy of **quietism** (*argumentum ad quietem*) is committed when it is argued or assumed that if no one complains, no one has anything to complain about. As Bentham put it: "Nobody complains, therefore nobody suffers". It is true, of course, that *one reason* a person might have for not complaining is that he is perfectly happy with his lot. However, another good reason for failing to complain is the fear of repercussions. This is surely one of the major reasons for the acquiescence of the owners of small businesses (laundries, restaurants, saloons, etc.) in the face of threats by crime syndicates. The syndicates make it very clear that they will not tolerate complaints; so the small businessmen suffer in silence.

A third good reason for suffering in silence is that complaints may be ineffectual. It may well be a waste of time, for instance, to complain to a winemaker about the evils of drinking. Similarly, there is not much future in complaining to a tyrant about the evils of his tyranny. Again, there are any number of cases symbolized by the proverbial "spilt milk" for which complaints would be completely ineffectual, e.g., we cannot raise the dead with complaints. Clearly, it would be a serious mistake to assume that no news is always good news or that a silent customer is always a satisfied one. This is the fallacy of *quietism*.

7.9 False consolation

The fallacy of **false consolation** is committed when it is claimed that as long as anyone's situation is worse than yours, yours is satisfactory. Like Job, we all have a few well-meaning friends who try to comfort us in our hour of need by assuring us that there are people who are much worse off. "Cheer up", they say, "things could have been much worse". And then they explain exactly how. While it may be true that short of complete annihilation things can always get much worse, that does not make anything bad *better*. A broken leg is not any more bearable if your neighbor has two broken legs. A soldier's freedom is not increased by the knowledge that prisoners have even less freedom. A young man's mobility is not increased by the knowledge that his father never had a car. Briefly, we might say that the fallacy of *false consolation* is committed by anyone who claims that the grass is *always browner* on the other side of the fence.

Review problems for Secs. 7.1–7.9

I. Distinguish the following forms of political fallacies:

1. the end justifies the means
2. no precedent
3. novelty
4. stagnation
5. imposter terms
6. special pleading
7. repeated assertion
8. quietism
9. false consolation

II. Name and explain the type of political fallacy involved in the following:

1. We believe in the economic principles of Karl Marx and we call ourselves The New Republicans.
2. You don't see anyone marching around in protest, do you? No demonstrations. No midnight meetings. That means nobody has any grievances.
3. SALESMAN: It's a smaller unit. It costs less to install. It looks better. What else can I say?
    PROSPECT: You forgot to mention the fact that it costs more to run.

4. I was hungry and he had food. That was reason enough to cut his throat.
5. That's really different. It must be good.
6. KING: We'll write it on their walls. We'll set it to music. We'll paint it on billboards, on the backs of cars and trucks. They'll believe it.
7. We've never had to keep our dog on a leash before, so we shouldn't have to now.
8. We've always had a stoplight on that corner, so it's time to take it down.
9. He wouldn't shut up. He kept calling me a *slob*. So I bashed his head in and that shut him up.
10. THIEF: I wouldn't say I stole from people. I would rather say I appropriated certain luxuries from those who had plenty and disseminated them to those who had none.
11. Just think about those guys in prison. They're a lot worse off than you.
12. That guy has been in office for twenty years. He has to be corrupt.
13. If you expect to get the job, you better forget about telling him you've been in jail. You don't have to lie about it. Just don't bring it up.
14. This is the first time I've heard that. It must be false.
15. This is the first time I've heard that. How can I reject it?
16. What do you mean he's unhappy? You don't hear *him* complaining, do you?
17. What are you complaining about? In China they don't even have a free press.

III. Make up examples of each of the fallacies distinguished in Part I.

7.10 Self-purification

The fallacy of **self-purification** is committed when it is assumed or argued that until one corrects all of one's own defects, one should not attempt to correct any others. No doubt you are familiar with the old saying that people who live in glass houses shouldn't throw stones. Presumably what this means is that people who are themselves blame-worthy should not criticize others. Within limits this is sound moral advice. But if the principle is interpreted so that only perfect people or people with perfect views or theories may properly criticize anyone or anything, the result is the elimination of all criticism. This must be considered a serious fallacy.

The growth and development of human knowledge and institutions would be severely curtailed if only perfect people or people with perfect views could criticize others or their views. If only saints were allowed the luxury of criticism, most blameworthy acts would go unchallenged, for there are many more of the latter than the former. Again, if only those with perfect scientific theories could criticize currently accepted theories, the progress of science would come to a complete halt. A perfect theory is not required in order to prove that some other theory is objectionable. If a theory leads to absurdities or false predictions, then it is in need of revision, whether or not anyone happens to have a better theory. Those who claim that all criticism must be withheld until a perfect theory is developed commit the fallacy of *self-purification*.

7.11 Procrastination

The fallacy of **procrastination** is committed when someone seems to be in favor of something (a policy change, the purchase of a new item, a new law, etc.) only if its appearance is *always* scheduled for some time in the future. This is a particularly useful and deceitful strategy for politicians. Suppose, for example, a constituent informs his representative that a swimming pool is needed in his district. The representative may commit the fallacy of *procrastination* by agreeing with his constituent in every aspect with the exception of the construction date. He may agree that a pool is definitely needed, that it should be large enough for a thousand children, that it should have so many diving boards, so many lifeguards. Point by point the representative might stand with his constituent—up to the construction date. At this point the representative would part company with his constituent. He might suggest that it is too early to be pressing for construction, or that other things have priority, or that the time is not right to ask for a pool. In short, he would commit himself to the project *in principle* but not *in fact*. In principle he would favor the construction of a new pool, but in fact the proper time to begin construction would never come.

The fallacy of *procrastination* is frequently committed on a somewhat smaller scale. The vast number of more or less intentionally unfulfilled promises (new cars and coats, vacations and parties, etc.) may be considered instances of this fallacy. Whenever anyone grants a request but persists in pushing the delivery date into the future, the fallacy of *procrastination* is committed.

7.12 Uncertain consequences

The fallacy of **uncertain consequences** is committed when it is erroneously supposed that there are so many *uncertain consequences* attached to the adoption of some new policy, program, or law that it must not be adopted. For example, suppose a certain kind of sewage disposal system is proposed for a town. Stanley Stopaction objects to it on the ground that it is bound to produce an unpleasant odor. After hearing a detailed explanation of the system's odor-preventing apparatus, Stanley still objects to it. Now, however, his view is simply that it is *too risky*. He is unable to specify *any* feature that might make it so, but he still insists that the system *could* produce unpredictable consequences which no one would want. Stanley has committed the fallacy of *uncertain consequences*. Similarly, one might have objected to the Medicare Bill and to Operation Headstart on the ground that they were bound to have some unpredictable and unattractive consequences. Certainly, no one could have known *a priori* if such novel social programs would have only the effects they were supposed to have or if they would raise more problems than they solved. But in the absence of any reliable data suggesting more harmful than helpful effects, such objections to the programs could only have been considered instances of the fallacy of *uncertain consequences*.

7.13   Creating doubts

The fallacy of **creating doubts** is committed when false rumors are spread about an issue or person to make people apprehensive or suspicious. Suppose, for instance, someone wants to block the sale of a piece of land to the city. Without openly attacking the issue, he can undermine it by spreading the rumor that whoever proposed purchasing the land stands to get a percentage of the sales price. Or, he might let it get around that the price of the property was raised as soon as the city became interested in it. Either or both rumors might be sufficient to have the purchase of the land shelved indefinitely.

Again, the fallacy of *creating doubts* might be committed by spreading rumors about a political candidate. If the candidate has a reputation for honesty, someone might circulate the rumor that the reputation was "bought with hard cash". If a particular newspaper supports the candidate, one might pass the word that it is a "payoff", i.e., that the candidate has made or intends to make some concession to the owners of the paper. Since the object of the fallacy is merely to *create a doubt*, which will then produce its own mischief, it is not necessary to elaborate on the rumors. Once suspicions, apprehensions, or misgivings are created, people will be misled by the old adage "where there is smoke, there is fire". Unfortunately, here both the smoke and the fire are imaginary.

7.14   Perfect world

The fallacy of the **perfect world** is committed when it is claimed that because certain laws, rules, or policies would be unnecessary in *a perfect world*, instead of enacting such laws, rules, or policies, we should try to develop a more *perfect world*. For example, instead of writing a constitution with checks and balances against the abuse of power, we should make sure that tyrants never get into positions of power. Instead of enacting more restrictive traffic laws, we should instruct drivers to be more careful. Instead of introducing stronger civil rights legislation, we should teach people not to be bigoted.

Those who commit the fallacy of the perfect world are guilty of only recommending action that would completely *eliminate* some evil, while rejecting all more or less *corrective* action. Although the former would be more thoroughgoing and would make the latter superfluous, the likelihood of creating a *perfect world* in some respect is nil, and the result of tackling such a task first is almost certain to be failure. What is worse, however, is that while time and other resources are being expended on a lost cause, the evils of the present world will continue to take their toll. That is to say, then, that the attempt to create a *perfect world* is likely to result in a more imperfect world which lacks even those remedial devices that tend to make the present world livable. It is difficult to imagine a politician (or anyone else, for that matter) making a more serious mistake.

7.15   Efficacy of time

It is a truism that many things change with time. As time passes people grow old, social institutions change, even physical environments change. To be more precise, we might say that time is a *necessary condition* of change, i.e., there can be no change without time, or change requires time. It is also a truism that many things remain fairly changeless with time. As time passes people remain trustworthy, dumb, or American;

some social institutions persist (people live in houses, wear clothes, etc.); and physical environments stay largely the same (rivers continue to run, mountains remain stable, etc.). In other and more technical words, we might say that time is not a *sufficient condition* of a particular change, i.e., there might well be a passage of time without some change, or time does not require change.

Now, the fallacy of the **efficacy of time** is committed when it is argued or assumed that the mere passage of time *must* bring about *significant* changes. While *some* changes might occur, they need not be significant. For example, consider the case of those who claim that there is no need for stronger civil rights legislation because time itself will bring about significant changes. This is a mistake. The only changes we can *count on* are insignificant so far as civil rights are concerned, e.g., the facts that people will continue to be born, grow old, and die are insignificant changes. Indeed, years might pass without any significant changes in the lives of minority groups such as Negroes and Indians. They might continue to be largely uneducated, unemployed or overworked, underpaid and underprivileged for many years to come.

Again, the fallacy of the *efficacy of time* is committed by those who believe that a student who spends twenty hours a week in a class must learn more than one who spends ten or five or none at all. This view seems to be based on a *faulty analogy*, i.e., it seems to be based on the idea that people are like sponges and that if they are "held under long enough they are bound to sop up something". Yet the most cursory inspection would reveal that people are much more like horses (or mules, if you will) than sponges, that the process by which one obtains an education is more like drinking than bathing, and finally, that the old adage about leading horses to water could just as well be about leading students to lectures.

7.16   Almighty will

One frequently hears it said that a man can do anything if he "really" wants to, and there is an old saying which runs: "Where there's a will, there's a way". When you stop and think about it, it almost seems miraculous that such blatant falsehoods have not been given a name by now. After all, everyone has *some* limitations. There is no *real* Superman and there are precious few Babe Ruths, Albert Einsteins, and Michelangelos. Hence, let us say that one who assumes or argues that a person can do anything if he "really" wants to, commits the fallacy of the **almighty will**. The *will*, if there is such a thing, is not *almighty*, as any fool can plainly see.

7.17   *Popular corruption*

The fallacy of **popular corruption** is committed by those who suppose that most people are little more than brutes and that, therefore, no matter how bad their lot is, they deserve it. For obvious reasons this is a fallacy committed more often in private than in public. Even in those countries in which the lives of large masses of people are manipulated by a handful of oligarchs, it would not be prudent to announce such a view publicly.

For a politician this is an extremely dangerous position to take. It is bound to breed negligence at best and severe oppression of the masses at worst. After all, no one is going to be particularly sensitive to the problems of people who are themselves presumed to be insensitive. Moreover, since there is no neat line separating the corrupt or corruptible from the incorrupt or incorruptible, those in power will be able to select those who deserve little or nothing just about as they please. This is tantamount to saying that those who commit the fallacy of *popular corruption* believe that those with enough *might* may do anything to anyone and it will turn out *right*. And *this*, I suppose, is about the greatest political fallacy of all.

Review problems for Secs. 7.10–7.17

I. Distinguish the following forms of political fallacies:

1. self-purification
2. procrastination
3. uncertain consequences
4. creating doubts
5. perfect world
6. efficacy of time
7. almighty will
8. popular corruption

II. Name and explain the type of political fallacy involved in the following:

1. The people, the people! Who cares about the people? Most of them are too dumb to know what's happening to them anyhow.
2. We don't need a law against water pollution. In time people will realize the need for clean water. Just wait.
3. I suppose *you* never did anything wrong?
4. How is anyone going to know the difference? Just say he's strange. The gossip will take care of the rest.
5. Sure they have a right to decent housing, but they have to go slow. They have to wait awhile.
6. If things were as they should be, we wouldn't need an army. So instead of sinking money into the army, why don't we just teach people to mind their own business.
7. You failed because you didn't want it badly enough. When someone really wants something, he gets it.
8. I don't have any specific reasons for opposing it. I just think it has too many loose ends. It's liable to create more problems than it solves.
9. A hundred years ago they were slaves. Just give it time. They'll get whatever is coming to them.
10. I don't know any citizens that are worth worrying about. They multiply like flies, and taken one at a time they're just about as important.
11. You've got the cart before the horse. First change their opinions, then you don't even have to change the law.
12. Sure my theory is inconsistent, but you have no right to criticize it because you don't even *have* a theory.
13. Try harder. It's always possible if you give it everything you've got.
14. When they ask you about him, you don't have to say anything. Just make a face, and let their dirty little minds do the rest.
15. RALFE: Next year is your year, baby. A new car, a new house; you name it; you got it.
    ALICE: Sure Ralfe, that's what you said last year.

III. Make up examples of each of the fallacies distinguished in Part I.

IV. Comprehensive review questions for this entire chapter: Name and explain the type of political fallacy involved in the following:

1. Sooner or later this corrupt regime will collapse. All we have to do is sit tight.
2. You have no room to complain about our short library hours. Some cities don't even *have* libraries.
3. You have been using that principle for twenty years. Don't you think it's time for a change?

4. Suppose something happens that we haven't expected. Are you willing to take the responsibility? I'm not. So I say we should do nothing.
5. Let's do it. It's new. It's different. It has to be good.
6. If manufacturers were more interested in producing high-quality merchandise instead of just high profits, there would be no need to worry about guarantees. So I say that instead of passing laws to strengthen guarantees, we should convince the manufacturers that their primary concern must be the quality of their products.
7. I know I said I was in favor of your bill, but I can't come out in support of it right now. Now is just not the right time.
8. HO: We intend to continue fighting until we have liberated all of our people.
   KY: We intend to continue fighting until we have punished all of the criminals.
9. Why should we throw away money on the masses. They're just a big blob of parasitic protoplasm.
10. BOLSHEVIK: It was necessary to eliminate the kulak class in order to realize our revolutionary goals.
11. How can you say he feels shut out? I'm his father and I've never heard him complain.
12. When you've got a *better* theory, you can criticize mine.
13. You've never done that before. It must be bad.
14. TYRANT: I want this slogan broadcast every hour on the hour, seven days a week. In a month they will be convinced it's true.
15. CANDIDATE: Now, I don't know what the incumbent does with his spare time, but he *does* seem to have more of it than most people, doesn't he?
16. White people don't need better schools. Only Negroes and Puerto Ricans need them.
17. All I know is that when people are oppressed they grumble. These people never grumble. So they're not oppressed.
18. Men, we're outnumbered twenty to one. But we'll beat 'em if you really want to.

chapter
eight   INDUCTIVE
FALLACIES

*It is preferable to try even in uncertainty
that not to try and be certain of getting
nothing.*   Hans Reichenbach

The conclusion of an inductive argument is supposed to be more or less acceptable relative to its premisses. When such an argument does not do what it is supposed to do, we may say an **inductive fallacy** has been committed. We have eight inductive fallacies to consider. With the exception of hasty generalization and the gambler's fallacy, which involve inductively invalid patterns, they are *informal* fallacies.

8.1   Hasty generalization

The fallacy of **hasty generalization** is committed when, after observing that a small number or a special sort of the members of some group have a given property, it is inferred that the whole group has this property. To put it in the language of the statisticians, we might say it is an inference from a quantitatively (insufficiently large) or qualitatively (peculiarly selected) unrepresentative sample to a whole population. Consider the following examples of *hasty generalizations* from *quantitatively* unrepresentative samples. First, someone infers that all Italians eat spaghetti on Saturdays from the fact that his Italian neighbor eats spaghetti on Saturdays. Again, he infers that a silver lure will work on all bass because it worked on one bass. Finally, he decides that all Plymouths are defective automobiles because his Plymouth is defective. His error is apparent. He makes a judgment about a population containing thousands of individuals on the basis of his observation of one. Actually, it is fairly certain that his *generalization* would have been practically as *hasty* if he had a sample of, say, five or six individuals. A mathematician or statistician could even give us a fairly precise estimate of its *degree* of hastiness (i.e., of its reliability or probable accuracy).

Examples of *hasty generalizations* from *qualitatively* unrepresentative samples might include the following. Someone infers that all the women in a hospital wear maternity dresses on the basis of his observation of some *pregnant* women in maternity dresses. He infers that everyone who stands on the corner of 9th Street and Hough Avenue begs, because some *panhandler* is doing it. He supposes that everyone is interested in directing traffic, because he has observed a *policeman* directing traffic. In short, his error is that he makes a judgment about a large population on the basis of his observation of certain members of that population who have very *special positions* or who happen to be in *extraordinary* or *atypical situations*.

8.2 Accident

The fallacy of **accident** (*fallacia accidentis*) is committed when a generalization or general principle is improperly applied to a single instance. For example, it is generally true that children ought to obey their parents. However, if Johnny's parents are psychopaths, it would surely be a mistake to insist that the injunction applies to Johnny. That is to say, Johnny's "accidental" circumstances are such that the principle is innapplicable. Hence, one who applies the principle to Johnny's case is committing a fallacy of *accident*.

Again, suppose a "loan shark" pointed out to his overdue debtor that a man ought to pay his debts and that insofar as he failed to pay his, he ought to expect punishment. Here is a perfectly good principle improperly applied. The principle should only be applied to legitimate creditors. If a man borrows money in good faith and is then confronted with the alternatives of paying an extraordinarily high interest rate or incurring, say, physical punishment, he is *not obliged* to meet either. If he has any moral obligation at all, it is to contact the police. Here the "loan shark" has committed the fallacy of *accident*.

The fallacy of *accident* is committed by lawyers, judges, and jurists who refuse to recognize mitigating circumstances when judging a person. Mitigating circumstances are, after all, accidents or additional elements in a situation which require special attention. When such elements are ignored, the result is likely to be a fallacy. The "letter" of the law is apt to be served without serving its "spirit".

8.3 False cause

The fallacy of appealing to a **false cause** is committed when some event is erroneously considered the cause of another event. In Latin the fallacy is known as *non causa pro causa*, i.e., mistaking what is not a cause for a cau. or *post hoc, ergo propter hoc*, i.e., after this, therefore because of this. If the term 'event' is defined loosely enough to include sentences, then this fallacy looks very much like the fallacy of *wrong reason*. But because sentences would be extremely peculiar events and because the fallacy of *false cause* might not involve an inaccurate application of a *reductio ad absurdum* argument, the two fallacies should be distinguished.

Let us consider a few examples. Suppose it rains immediately after you wash your car. If you claim that the washing of your car is the cause of the rain, you commit the fallacy of *false cause*. Again, it has been reported that many great Indian philosophers have spent ten minutes every morning doing headstands. The fallacy of *false cause* is committed if a man claims that their greatness is the result of their headstands. Finally, it might be argued fallaciously that Napoleon's stature was the cause of his becoming an emperor.

Insofar as superstitions are related to causal connections, the appeal to a superstition is an appeal to a *false cause*. Hence, we might call such an appeal an *argumentum ad superstitionem*, i.e., an appeal to *superstition*. For example, if someone claims that you are bound to meet with misfortune because a black cat crossed your path, or you broke a mirror, or you walked under a ladder, etc., he is appealing to *superstition* or to a *false cause*. Knocking on wood to prevent misfortune is another instance of this fallacy.

8.4 Gambler's

According to the classical theory of measuring probabilities, when a "fair" coin is flipped there is a probability of 1 in 2 that a head will turn up

There are only two possibilities, and one of them is a head. If a coin is flipped twice, the probability of a head turning up both times is $\frac{1}{2} \times \frac{1}{2} = \frac{1}{4}$. The probability of three flips turning up three heads is $\frac{1}{2} \times \frac{1}{2} \times \frac{1}{2} = \frac{1}{8}$. Quite generally, the greater the number of flips the smaller the probability that they will *all* be heads. The turning up of a head (or a tail) when a coin is flipped is called a **chance event**. Another example of a chance event is the turning up of a face with six dots on it when an "unloaded" die is tossed. If we happen to get, say, two heads in two flips of a coin we say a **run** of two heads has occurred. If the face with six dots turns up three times in three tosses, we say a run of three sixes has turned up, and so on.

When someone argues that because a *chance* event has had a certain run in the past, the probability of its occurrence in the future is significantly altered, he commits the **gambler's** fallacy. Sometimes it is called the fallacy of **maturing chances**. For example, suppose you have flipped a "fair" coin five times and it has turned up heads every time. After such a long run of heads, you might think that the chances of a tail occurring on the next toss are now *better* than 1 in 2. If so, you would be committing the gambler's fallacy. Each toss of the coin is *independent* of every other and has no effect on it. So, no matter how long a run of heads you have, the chances of a tail turning up on the next toss are unchanged. If the chance of a tail turning up on the first toss is 1 in 2 then it is still 1 in 2 after any number of heads (or tails). That's part of what we mean by a chance event.

Flips of a "fair" coin and tosses of an "unloaded" die are independent occurrences. What happens on *this* flip or toss has no effect on what happens on *that* one. On the other hand, when someone draws a card from an ordinary deck of playing cards, that *can* have an effect on the chances of certain other occurences. For example, the chances of drawing an ace from such a deck are 4 in 52. However, if *I* draw an ace and do not replace it, then *you* only have 3 chances in 51 of drawing one. Of course, if I replace my ace, then the chances of your drawing one are again 4 in 52. People who commit the gambler's fallacy seem to believe that the chance events they bet on are like the card case *without* replacement, when in fact those events are like the card case *with* replacement.

8.5   *Faulty analogy*

Two things are said to be **analogous** insofar as they are similar Thus, a heart is analogous to a pump insofar as it is similar to a pump. An umbrella is analogous to a tree insofar as it is similar to a tree. There is an analogy between the supreme ruler of a state and the captain of a ship insofar as there is a similarity between the two. In an **argument by analogy**, one argues that because two things are analogous or similar in some respects, it is *likely* that they are similar in some other or others. Schematically, analogical arguments might be represented as follows:

> Object *a* has properties *P, Q, R, S*, and *T*.
> Object *b* has properties *P, Q, R, S*.
> ────────────────────
> It is *likely* that *b* also has *T*.

For example, consider the following:

> Object *a* has a brain, talks, writes, reads, and thinks.
> Object *b* has a brain, talks, writes, and reads.
> ────────────────────
> It is *likely* that *b* also thinks.

This sort of argument may be muddled in at least two ways. A fallacy of **faulty analogy** is committed if (1) the conclusion of an analogical argument is considered certain, or (2) the analogous things have more *differences* than similarities. Let us consider each of these cases more carefully.

(1) In the first place, a fallacy of faulty analogy is committed if one assumes that the conclusion of an analogical argument is certain and not merely more or less acceptable. Analogical arguments are a type of inductive argument. Hence, by definition, their conclusions are only more or less acceptable.

(2) Frequently a *faulty analogy* occurs because two things which have some similarities have even *more* differences. Suppose, for instance, it is claimed that professional fighters are like racehorses. There are certain similarities between fighters and racehorses. The success of either is a function of their strength, training, spirit, and good fortune. But there are many more *important differences* which are apt to be disguised by this simile. For example, it might be supposed that fighters are insensitive to human problems, that they do not need friends, that they do not have hopes or dreams, that they may be "turned out to pasture", as it were, when they are too old to compete. In short, the *needs* of fighters are quite different from those of racehorses. Hence, one would be committing a serious fallacy of *faulty analogy* if one inferred on the basis of their similarities that, say, we have no more responsibility to fighters than we do to racehorses. Too often this is exactly the sort of inference that has been made about professional athletes.

8.6   Central tendency

Suppose a class of seven students is given a spelling test and the scores are recorded as follows:

20   11   5   4   3   3   3

The **arithemetic mean** of a set of numbers is found by adding them and dividing the total by the number of numbers in the set. For our example, we divide 49 by 7 and get 7. The **mode** of a set of numbers is the value that occurs most frequently. For our example the mode is 3. Finally, the **median** is the value of the middle number when the whole set is arranged in descending order from the highest to lowest. The median of the set of numbers above is 4.

Means, medians, and modes are known as **measures of central tendencies**. They indicate the tendency of a set of numbers to "cluster about" this or that value in one way or another. They are often used as very brief summaries of sets of numbers, and when they are used improperly or misleadingly, we say that a fallacy of **central tendency** has been committed. For example, suppose an employer says that his five employees (all of whom are equally deserving) should not complain about their salaries because they are "averaging" $6,000 a year. If they have a **mean** salary of $6,000 but the distribution looks like this:

$26,000 $1,000 $1,000 $1,000 $1,000

then four employees have plenty to complain about. In this case, either the *median* or the *mode* $1,000 would have been a more accurate summary of the situation. When the employer used the arithmetic mean to summarize the salaries, he committed a fallacy of *central tendency*.

Again, suppose the following distribution of test scores is summarized by reporting that the average score is 60:

1   3   3   3   3   4   60   90   94   94   94   94   97

The *median is* 60, but this is hardly an accurate summary of the thirteen scores. Most people either scored very low 3 or very high 94. Hence, it would be misleading to report a mode of 3 *or* of 94. To avoid committing a fallacy of central tendency, we should say that the distribution has *two* modes or is **bimodal** about 3 and 94. So-called memory courses frequently yield distributions of test scores that are bimodal in character, because those who memorize the material have no trouble at all, and those who fail to memorize the material are completely lost.

8.7 Misleading percentages

N percent of any number equals $\frac{N}{100}$ times that number. For example, 5 percent of 80 is $\frac{5}{100}$ times 80, or 4. 6 percent of 90 equals $\frac{6}{100}$ times 90, or 5.4, and so on. The fallacy of **misleading percentages** is committed when someone tries to support a view by citing a misleading percentage. For example, suppose your car has been at a mechanic's garage for a week. You telephone him and ask why there has been such a delay. He tells you that there is no problem because he has been able to put in *twice* as much time on it today as he has all week. This is an increase of attention equal to *two hundred percent*, and that sounds like action. However, if he worked on your car only two minutes yesterday and four today, then what he has said is highly misleading. Instead, his claim must be regarded as a fallacy of *misleading percentages*.

Again, suppose a candidate for some political office claims that the incumbent is unacceptable because under the latter's leadership the numbers of local suicides has increased 100 percent. Aside from the obvious fact that there may be no connection between the suicides and the government, the percentage increase may be less informative than the *total* increase. If there were two suicides this year and one last year, there would be an increase of 100 percent, but not a very shocking increase. The misleading reference to the percentage increase should be regarded as a fallacy.

8.8 Misleading totals

The fallacy of **misleading totals** is roughly the opposite of the fallacy of misleading percentages. That is, when someone cites the total number of occurrences of a certain event when it is likely to be more misleading than a reference to a percentage or a proportion, we say a fallacy of *misleading totals* has been committed. For example, someone might claim that because there are more automobile accidents in the daytime than at night, it is safer to drive at night. In this case it would be better to know the percentage of accidents occurring in the daytime and at night. If, say, 20 percent of "night" drivers suffer accidents compared to, say, 5 percent of "day" drivers then (from the statistical point of view) it is safer to drive in the daytime.

Similarly, a pharmaceutical company might claim that more people are cured by its drug than by any other, although the percentage of cures by *any* drug is insignificant. If *any* drug can be expected to be effective, say, 1 percent of the time, while drug X is effective $1\frac{1}{2}$ percent of the time, then very little can be said for drug X *or* the others. The claim that drug X cures more people than any other merely disguises the fact that all of the drugs are practically ineffective. This would be a fallacy of *misleading totals*.

Review problems for Secs. 8.1–8.8

I.   Distinguish the following forms of inductive fallacy:

1. hasty generalization
2. accident
3. false cause
4. gambler's
5. faulty analogy
6. central tendency
7. misleading percentages
8. misleading totals

II. Name and explain the type of inductive fallacy involved in each of the following:

1. This is a free country, isn't it? So what's yours is mine.
2. What do you mean "Not all Negroes carry knives"? I saw one carrying a knife the other day.
3. I wouldn't try to become a star without a moustache. After all, even Gable couldn't have made it without one.
4. Women grow up, but men are like little boys all their lives.
5. I'm really hitting the books this year. I have increased my study time 100 percent.
6. The wheel has hit a black square twelve times in a row. Red is bound to turn up next.
7. The average value of houses in Poorsville is $8000, so most of them are probably okay.
8. Did you see that woman go through the red light? Boy, women drivers are really pathetic.

9. Nobody can criticize our administration, because we made fewer mistakes this year than last.
10. I don't care if he did weigh three times as much as you. A good scout *always* tries to help. You should have jumped in and tried to save him.
11. I'm telling you it will rain. It rains every time I decide to go fishing.
12. Women are like buses. So one is as good as another as long as she's available and headed in the right direction.
13. MERT: Just how much success are you having out there?
    BERT: Twice as much as last year.
14. Even if I replace my card after each draw, the law of averages says I have to get a winner sooner or later.
15. Never mind modes and medians, the only sure indicator is the arithmetic mean.
16. Everyone there went for the idea. What more support could you want.
17. I was so sick after I ate those green apples that I swore I would never eat another apple again.
18. Knock on wood; otherwise you'll have bad luck.
19. I've only known one union representative and he was a louse. I wouldn't trust any of them.
20. Children are like animals. All they need is food, a place to sleep, and a pen to play in.

III. Make up examples of each of the fallacies distinguished in Part I.

Suggestions for further reading

Bentham, Jeremy, *The Handbook of Political Fallacies.* New York: Harper & Row Publishers, 1962.

Carney, James D., and Richard K. Scheer, *Fundamentals of Logic.* New York: The Macmillan Company, 1964, Chapters 1, 2, 4-6.

Fearnside, W. Ward, and William B. Holther, *Fallacy: The Counterfeit of Argument.* Englewood Cliffs, N.J.: Prentice-Hall, Inc., 1959.

Hepp, Maylon H., *Thinking Things Through.* New York: Charles Scribner's Sons, 1956, Chapters 3, 5, and 31.

Little, Winston W., W. Harold Wilson, and W. Edgar Moore, *Applied Logic.* Boston: Houghton Mifflin Company, 1955. Part I.

Schipper, Edith Watson, and Edward Schuh, *A First Course in Modern Logic.* New York: Holt, Rinehart & Winston, Inc., 1960, Chapters 5-9.

Thouless, Robert H., *How to Think Straight.* New York: Simon and Schuster, Inc., 1939.

ANSWERS
TO
REVIEW
QUESTIONS

1.2:V

1. f	6. f	11. t	16. t
2. f	7. t	12. f	17. f
3. f	8. f	13. f	
4. t	9. f	14. f	
5. f	10. f	15. t	

1.3:II–III

II.
1. v	7. v
2. I	8. v
3. v	9. v
4. I	10. I
5. I	11. I
6. I	12. I

III.
1. v	7. NA
2. NA	8. V
3. I	9. V
4. V	10. NA
5. V	11. V
6. V	12. V

1.4:III

1. fda	6. t	11. n	16. am
2. am	7. n	12. n	17. fda
3. n	8. dm	13. cd	18. t
4. dm	9. fac	14. t	19. fac
5. cd	10. t	15. n	

2:II

1. assume every instance
2. circular definition
3. circular reasoning
4. alleged certainty
5. equivalent expressions
6. assume more general claim
7. epithets
8. complex question

9. alleged certainty
10. circular definition
11. assume every instance
12. equivalent expressions
13. epithets
14. complex questions
15. circular reasoning

3.1–3.8:II

1. confident manner
2. tradition
3. popular sentiments
4. jargon
5. popular people
6. aphorisms
7. titles
8. ceremony

9. popular sentiments
10. jargon
11. titles
12. tradition
13. confident manner
14. aphorisms
15. ceremony

3.9–3.16:II

1. misrepresented authority
2. apriorism
3. irrelevant authority
4. large numbers
5. imaginary authority
6. faith
7. self-interest
8. idols

9. misrepresented authority
10. irrelevant authority
11. idols
12. faith
13. apriorism
14. large numbers
15. imaginary authority

3.9–3.16:IV

1. popular sentiments
2. apriorism
3. circular definition
4. tradition
5. circular reasoning
6. assume every instance
7. self-interest
8. popular people
9. equivalent expressions
10. alleged certainty
11. faith

       .eral claim

14. imaginary authority
15. irrelevant authority
16. jargon
17. epithets
18. misrepresented authority
19. aphorisms
20. large numbers
21. ceremony
22. complex questions
23. titles
24. idols
25. popular sentiments

·4.8:II

1. bad connections
2. you're another
3. ignorance
4. abusing man
5. force
6. pity
7. bad seed
8. faulty motives

9. you're another
10. ignorance
11. bad connections
12. abusing man
13. pity
14. force
15. faulty motives

4.9–4.14:II

1. friendship
2. is-ought
3. attacking illustrations
4. fear
5. wrong reason
6. wishful thinking

7. attacking illustrations
8. fear
9. friendship
10. wishful thinking
11. is-ought

4.15–4.21:II

1. simple diversion
2. vacuous guarantee
3. good intentions
4. straw man
5. Monday morning quarterback
6. pride
7. rationalization
8. simple diversion
9. vacuous guarantee
10. straw man
11. pride
12. Monday morning quarterback
13. rationalization
14. simple diversion
15. good intentions

4.15–4.21:IV

1. wishful thinking
2. you're another
3. simple diversion
4. fear
5. pride
6. is-ought
7. ignorance
8. faulty motives
9. Monday morning quarterback
10. wrong reason
11. good intentions
12. force
13. vacuous guarantee
14. abusing man
15. attacking illustrations
16. bad seed
17. rationalization
18. friendship
19. bad connections
20. straw man
21. pity
23. simple diversion
22. ignorance

5.1–5.7:II

1. contradictory assumptions
2. lack understanding
3. anger
4. amphiboly
5. accent
6. equivocation
7. anger
8. accent
9. humor
10. anger
11. lack understanding
12. equivocation
13. accent
14. amphiboly
15. contradictory assumptions
16. humor
17. equivocation

5.8–5.14:II

1. etymology
2. question–question
3. psuedoarguments
4. trivial objections
5. exception to rule
6. emotional language
7. question–question
8. alleged ambiguity
9. pseudoarguments
10. etymology
11. trivial objections
12. exception to rule
13. alleged ambiguity
14. emotional language
15. alleged ambiguity
16. trivial objections

5.8–5.14:IV

1. amphiboly
2. exceptions to rule
3. alleged ambiguity
4. lack understanding
5. emotional language
6. question–question
7. accent
8. trivial objections
9. humor
10. etymology
11. equivocation
12. anger
13. amphiboly
14. pseudoarguments
15. alleged ambiguity

6:II

1. golden mean
2. vague terms
3. false dilemma
4. illicit contrast
5. division
6. composition
7. continuum
8. vague terms
9. illicit contrast
10. oversimplification
11. golden mean
12. false dilemma
13. illicit contrast
14. composition
15. division
16. oversimplification
17. continuum

7.1–7.9:II

1. imposter terms
2. quietism
3. special pleading
4. end justifies means
5. novelty
6. repeated assertions
7. no precedent
8. stagnation
9. end justifies means

10. imposter terms
11. false consolation
12. stagnation
13. special pleading
14. no precedent
15. novelty
16. quietism
17. false consolation

7.10–7.17:II

1. popular corruption
2. efficacy of time
3. self-purification
4. creating doubts
5. procrastination
6. perfect world
7. almighty will
8. uncertain consequences

9. efficacy of time
10. popular corruption
11. perfect world
12. self-purification
13. almighty will
14. creating doubts
15. procrastination

7.10–7.17:IV

1. efficacy of time
2. false consolation
3. stagnation
4. uncertain consequences
5. novelty
6. perfect world
7. procrastination
8. imposter terms
9. popular corruption

10. end justifies means
11. quietism
12. self-purification
13. no precedent
14. repeated assertions
15. creating doubts
16. special pleading
17. quietism
18. almighty will

8:II

1. accident
2. hasty generalization
3. false cause
4. faulty analogy
5. misleading percentages
6. gambler's
7. central tendency
8. hasty generalization
9. misleading total
10. accident

11. false cause
12. faulty analogy
13. misleading percentage
14. gambler's
15. central tendency
16. misleading total
17. hasty generalization
18. false cause
19. hasty generalization
20. faulty analogy

INDEX

123